FOREX INVESTING DISSECTED

A GUIDE TO SUCCESSFUL TRADING

DR. K. Aizaz

Copyright © 2013 Dr. Khawar Aizaz

All rights reserved. No part of this book may be reproduced in any form without written permission from the publisher and author. Except for use in any review, the reproduction or utilization of this work in whole or in part in any form by an electronic, mechanical or other means, now known or hereafter invented, including photocopying, recording, or any information storage or retrieval system, is forbidden without the written permission of the publisher and author.

Published By:

K & K Houston Publishing
P.O. Box 836
Dumfries, VA 22026-0836
www.kkhoustonpublishing.com

ISBN: 978-0-9796524-8-6
Library of Congress Control Number: 2013917938

PRINTED IN THE USA

This book is dedicated to my lovely wife Hina and my precious kids Farah and Zeeshan

PREFACE

Forex Investing is a relatively new concept and over the last decade Forex trading has developed into the world's largest market. Forex is larger than any bond and equity market worldwide and is traded 24 hours per day for five days a week. The intended audiences for "Forex Investing Dissected – *A Guide to Successful Trading*" are undergraduates, graduates, professionals, traders, retirees, investors and any individual who is involved in trading stocks and bonds.

Lack of awareness has prevented general populous any access to the Forex markets. The purpose of this work is to create awareness, define concepts, describe strategies and lay down expectations about Forex Trading for the global audience. I foresee a tremendous potential for my work as Forex education has not been attempted before in such a practical format.

New and prospective Forex traders are at a huge disadvantage as there is a paucity of quality literature on Forex trading, the books available are limited and quite vague and focus on theories of market functions without tying it to the day to day trading information that a trader requires.

Therefore, I took it upon myself to study the Forex market in details and find solutions to the problems in order to make Forex Trading accessible to common man and make this experience rewarding and worthwhile.

Acknowledgements

This work would not have been possible without the excellent FOREX educational material made available by Oanda Corporation ®, and FOREX Factory ®. I have been able to reference the excellent FOREX charts and platforms with permission for educational purposes in my work.

Thank you

Risk Disclosures

Remember there is a substantial risk of loss in futures and Forex trading. Past performance is not indicative of future results. Do not trade with money you cannot afford to lose. Please carefully consider whether such trading is suitable for you in light of your financial condition. You should read, understand, and consider the Risk Disclosure Statement that is provided by your broker before you consider trading.

Online trading is risky. *The risk of loss in online trading of stocks, options, and foreign equities is substantial.*

In addition, hypothetical trading does not involve financial risk, and no hypothetical trading record can completely account for the impact of financial risk in actual trading. The trading methods and sample trades listed in this book are for educational purposes only and should not be construed in any way as trading advice.

LIMIT OF LIABILITY / DISCLAIMER OF WARRANTY

THE PUBLISHER AND THE AUTHOR MAKE NO REPRESENTATIONS OR WARRANTIES WITH RESPECT TO THE ACCURACY OR COMPLETENESS OF THE CONTENTS OF THIS WORK AND SPECIFICALLY DISCLAIM ALL WARRANTIES, INCLUDING WITHOUT LIMITATION WARRANTIES OF FITNESS FOR A PARTICULAR PURPOSE. NO WARRANTY MAY BE CREATED OR EXTENDED BY SALES OR PROMOTIONAL MATERIALS. THE ADVICE AND STRATEGIES CONTAINED HEREIN MAY NOT BE SUITABLE FOR EVERY SITUATION. THIS WORK IS SOLD WITH THE UNDERSTANDING THAT THE PUBLISHER IS NOT ENGAGED IN RENDERING LEGAL, ACCOUNTING, OR OTHER PROFESSIONAL SERVICES. IF PROFESSIONAL ASSISTANCE IS REQUIRED, THE SERVICES OF A COMPETENT PROFESSIONAL PERSON SHOULD BE SOUGHT. NEITHER THE PUBLISHER NOR THE AUTHOR SHALL BE LIABLE FOR DAMAGES ARISING HERE FROM. THE FACT THAT AN ORGANIZATION

OR WEBSITE IS REFERRED TO IN THIS WORK AS A CITATION AND/OR A POTENTIAL SOURCE OF FURTHER INFORMATION DOES NOT MEAN THAT THE AUTHOR OR THE PUBLISHER ENDORSES THE INFORMATION THE ORGANIZATION OR WEBSITE MAY PROVIDE OR RECOMMENDATIONS IT MAY MAKE.

FURTHER, READERS SHOULD BE AWARE THAT INTERNET WEBSITES LISTED IN THIS WORK MAY HAVE CHANGED OR DISAPPEARED BETWEEN WHEN THIS WORK WAS WRITTEN AND WHEN IT IS READ.

TABLE OF CONTENTS

Chapter 1: Introduction   1
Forex Defined   3

Chapter 2: Basics   7
   Currency Pairs   9

Chapter 3: Forex Terminology   13
Percentage in Points (PIPS)   15
Spread   15
Trading Lots   18
 Leverage and Margin   20
 Forex Charts   22

Chapter 4: Fundamentals Impacting Currencies   27
Trade Flow   29
Balance of Trade   29
Gross Domestic Product (GDP)   29
Manufacturing Indices   29
Industrial Production   30
Flow of Capital   30
Interest Rates/Central Banks Meetings   30
Consumer Price Index (CPI)   30
Producer Price Index (PPI)   30
Consumer Confidence Reports   30
Labor Report   30

Chapter 5: Technical Trading   33
Trend   35
Visual Identification of the Trend   35
Characteristics of an Up-trend   37
Characteristics of a Downtrend   38
Identification of the Trend by using a Moving Average   39
Use of a Single SMA to determine the Trend   40
Use of a Multiple SMA's to determine the Trend   41

Support and Resistance	42
Support	42
Resistance	43
Fibonacci Retracements	48
Candlestick Patterns	50
Normal Candlesticks	50
Simple Candlestick Patterns	51
Complex Candlestick Patterns	54
Indicators	58
Relative Strength Index (RSI)	60
Price Patterns	63
Head and Shoulders	64
Reverse Head and Shoulders	65
Pennants	66
Ascending Triangle	67
Descending Triangle	67
Bull Flag	68
Bear Flag	69
Double Top or Bottom	70
Triple Top or Bottom	72
Chapter 6: Practical Applications	**74**
Demo Account Broker # 1	82
Sample Demo Trade # 1	101
Sample Demo Trade # 2	106
Chapter 7: Key to Success	**113**
Expectations	115
Steps to Magical Trading	123
The Beginning	134
Answers to Quizzes	135

INTRODUCTION

CHAPTER ONE

Disclaimer*: The content on this page is for educational purposes only and should not be construed in any way as trading advice. The risk of loss in online trading of stocks, Forex, options, and foreign equities is substantial.*

INTRODUCTION

FOREX DEFINED:

Forex is a term used commonly to represent Foreign Exchange. This exchange allows individuals and investors to trade various currencies.

Forex market is larger than any bond and equity market and is also the most liquid in the world. It is open for trading 24 hours a day, five days a week and is accessible to investors trading a few hundred dollars to investors trading millions of dollars at a time.

The value of one currency in relation to another currency is called the exchange rate between those currencies. This exchange rate is very dynamic and changes many times during the day therefore allowing the investors an opportunity to profit from these moves. Later on in this book we will identify various factors which determine valuation of one currency against another.

Most of us at some stage in our life have carried out these transactions as we travel around the globe or as part of our business commitments in various countries.

In May 2009 I had a chance to visit my friend and family in UK. I flew into Heathrow airport in London. My friend, John was at the airport to receive me. I picked up my bags and went over to the currency exchange counter as I had some $ 2000 to change over to British Pounds. As the exchange rate that day was 1.34 dollars to a pound, my $2000 equaled 1492.5 pounds. After paying 5% in commission and fees I netted approximately 1418 pounds in cash. I stayed with John in Ilford, Essex, a small county outside London for a couple of days and then left for Edinburgh, Scotland to spend some time with my distant relatives whom I have not seen for about 15 years. The drive from London to Edinburgh was truly amazing, especially the scenery across the Cumbria region. I was due back in Houston, TX in August of 2009. A day before my departure to Houston, I drove back to London and stayed overnight at my friend's house.

The next day John dropped me at Heathrow airport, prior to checking-in I realized that I have about 1300 pounds left over which I needed to exchange back to dollars, therefore I went to the currency exchange counter in the departures lounge. During the last four months the pound had appreciated considerably and the exchange rate offered was 1.71 dollars to a pound. After paying another 5% in commission and fees I got $2112 in cash for the 1300 pounds left over. I was ecstatic that after spending nearly 200 pounds and paying 5% in commission and fees I had $112 more than what I started with. This was possible due to fluctuation in the pound/dollar exchange rate over the last three months. It would be impractical if we have to go to the airport every time we consider executing a Forex transaction, but using the same principles I want to introduce, from the comforts of your home via an electronic trading platform, a complex but an intriguing world of Forex investing.

It is getting a bit chilly here in my study, while I close the window and get myself a warm blanket I will leave you with an exercise to complete.

Quiz A:

> *My friend, John calls me and asks for a loan of $10000 as he is buying a restaurant in Munich, Germany. He requests that the money be sent to his account in Germany. I wire transfer him the amount through my bank here in Houston. The bank quotes me an exchange rate of 1.20 dollars to a Euro. John keeps his promise and returns the loan after six months. He exactly returns the amount he received in Euros; the day he wired the money back to me, his bank in Munich offered him an exchange rate of 1.60 dollars to a Euro. Please determine how many Euros did John receive, and upon return how many dollars were credited to my account. For simplicity sake let's assume that there were no wire fees or commissions charged during this transaction.*
>
> *1. $10000 sent to John at a rate of 1.20 = 10000 divided by 1.20 as we are changing dollars to euros = _____*

Disclaimer: *The content on this page is for educational purposes only and should not be construed in any way as trading advice. The risk of loss in online trading of stocks, Forex, options, and foreign equities is substantial.*

(2). John receives = _____ Euros

(3). John sends back _____ Euros at a rate of 1.60 =

(4). $ _____ (multiply answer for # 3 by 1.60 as now we are changing Euros to dollars)

(5). My account is credited with = _____ dollars

If you receive more than what you transferred over, then give yourself a pat on the back as that is the correct answer. If your account shows a lesser amount than what was transferred over then redo the exercise over.

The following chapter deals with the basic set up of currency pairs followed by chapters on terminology, fundamentals impacting currency valuations, technical trading, practical set up and applications of Forex investing and finally money management and taking charge, as we embark upon exploring the limitless opportunities of investing in Forex.

Disclaimer: *The content on this page is for educational purposes only and should not be construed in any way as trading advice. The risk of loss in online trading of stocks, Forex, options, and foreign equities is substantial.*

BASICS

CHAPTER TWO

Disclaimer*: The content on this page is for educational purposes only and should not be construed in any way as trading advice. The risk of loss in online trading of stocks, Forex, options, and foreign equities is substantial.*

BASICS

CURRENCY PAIRS:

In Forex, currencies are paired together. In order to buy the US dollars another currency has to be sold and vice versa.

      e.g.: USD   VS CAD
            United States Dollar vs. Canadian Dollar
            This pair is represented as USD/CAD

The currencies for both USA and Canada are called Dollar, though both these dollars have a different valuation.

Let's familiarize ourselves with some currency pairs:

        EUR/USD Euro / US Dollar
        GBP/USD Great Britain Pound / US Dollar
        USD/JPY   US Dollar / Japanese Yen
        USD/CHF US Dollar / Switzerland Franc
        NZD/USD New Zealand Dollar / US Dollar
        AUD/USD Australian Dollar / US Dollar
        USD/MXN US Dollar / Mexican Peso
        EUR/JPY   Euro / Japanese Yen
        GBP/CHF Great Britain Pound / Switzerland Franc

EUR/USD is the most commonly traded pair; therefore it provides multiple trading opportunities throughout the day. In addition GBP/USD, USD/CHF & USD/JPY are the other pairs which constitute majority of the trading daily. These four commonly traded pairs are called "Majors" and some Forex traders confine themselves to these majors only.

The currency pairs which do not have US dollar as one of the currency e.g. EUR/JPY are called "Crosses". The pairs you decide to trade are up to you.

Disclaimer: The content on this page is for educational purposes only and should not be construed in any way as trading advice. The risk of loss in online trading of stocks, Forex, options, and foreign equities is substantial.

Quiz Time:

    A. From the currency pairs listed above create 5 crosses:

        1. _____EUR/CHF_____
        2. _____
        3. _____
        4. _____
        5. _____

    B. List 5 more currency pairs:

        1. _____USD/HKD_____
        2. _____
        3. _____
        4. _____
        5. _____

    C. Name the currencies along with currency abbreviations for the following countries:

        1. South Africa = Rand,   ZAR

        2. France = _____

Disclaimer: The content on this page is for educational purposes only and should not be construed in any way as trading advice. The risk of loss in online trading of stocks, Forex, options, and foreign equities is substantial.

3. Sweden = _____

4. Hungary = _____

5. Turkey = _____

As you may have noticed each currency is represented by three upper case letters, in addition certain pairs have dollars listed first e.g. USD/CHF or USD/CAD, while certain pairs have dollar as a denominator e.g. EUR/USD or AUD/USD. The first currency within a pair is called the "base currency" while the second currency is termed the "quote currency". Which currency will be the base and which one will be a quote is determined by International Standardization Organization (ISO). This allows for ease in communication between traders and investors but does not in any way impact the value or performance of the currency pair.

Two investors are discussing an impact of interest rate changes announced by the Swiss National Bank (SNB) on the USD/CHF pair. In light of these changes they foresee the pair moving up from the current value of 0.92 and they will be entering long this pair. Basically it means that they foresee dollar strengthening against the Swiss franc, therefore they will buy the dollar and sell the franc. In the coming few weeks the pair appreciates to 0.95, at that level they close their trade by selling the dollars and buying back the francs they sold at 0.92 levels thereby making a reasonable profit. Lack of standardization will create confusion in the above mentioned scenario. The trader using USD as the base will profit while the trader who has switched the pair around e.g. CHF/USD will end up buying the francs and therefore suffering a loss, as both traders were talking about entering long this pair.

Disclaimer: The content on this page is for educational purposes only and should not be construed in any way as trading advice. The risk of loss in online trading of stocks, Forex, options, and foreign equities is substantial.

Going long means buying the base currency and selling the quote currency, which is in anticipation of the base currency within the pair to appreciate, while going short means selling the base currency and buying the quote currency, which is in anticipation of the quote currency within the pair to appreciate.

Ready for a short quiz again, Let us begin.

Quiz D

1. AUD/USD   The base currency is _____ and the quote currency is _____
2. USD/CAD   The base currency is _____ and the quote currency is _____
3. I am long the USD/JPY pair Which currency I bought _____
4. I am short the GBP/JPY pair   Which currency I sold _____
5. I entered long in the NZD/USD pair at 81.45, after about a week the pair is trading at 81.25, did I profit or did I lose money on my trade? _____

EUR/USD is currently trading at 1.29, what it means is that 1 Euro equals 1.29 dollars, or in technical terms the base currency in this pair, which is euro, is more valuable than the quote currency of the pair i.e. dollar at this given time.

$$EUR/USD = 1.29$$
$$EUR \quad : USD$$
$$1 \quad\quad : 1.29$$

If we want to determine how many euros is one dollar equal to, then we set up the equation as follows:

$$EUR/USD = 1/1.29 = 0.775$$
Therefore 1 dollar equals 0.775 euros

I hope you are still with me and not lost in the math, it is okay if you don't understand the calculations, we will have a few more problems to solve before we wrap up this chapter. Let us stretch ourselves a bit before diving into the next chapter. There is still a lot of interesting material to cover.

Quiz E

1. Currently GBP/USD is trading at 1.60. Please determine the following:
   1 Pound = _____ Dollars
   1 Dollar = _____ Pounds

2. Currently USD/CHF is trading at 0.92. Please determine the following:
   1 Dollar = _____ Swiss Francs
   1 Swiss Franc = _____ Dollars

Disclaimer: *The content on this page is for educational purposes only and should not be construed in any way as trading advice. The risk of loss in online trading of stocks, Forex, options, and foreign equities is substantial.*

FOREX TERMINOLOGY

CHAPTER THREE

FOREX TERMINOLOGY

PERCENTAGE IN POINTS (PIP):

Each currency has a smallest unit of denomination, which in the case of US dollar it is a cent, also referred to as one penny. The prices are quoted in dollars and cents e.g. a gallon of milk costs us 3 dollars and 48 cents and is listed as 3.48 dollars. In Forex trading however the decimal is carried out two more places. In chapter two I mentioned that EUR/USD is trading at 1.29 but in actual fact it was trading at 1.2973. The last number which is one hundredth of a penny is called a PIP. The movements in the currency pair are recorded in pips and based upon the value of a pip, a profit or a loss in a particular trade is determined. Some trading platforms will show five digits after the decimal which represents a tenth of a pip, but for all practical reasons we will ignore this fifth digit in our investing. Later on within this chapter we will learn about how the cost of a pip is determined

SPREAD:

If you look at the GBP/USD pair above, you will see two prices being displayed. The sell price which is also called "Ask" is 1.6483 and the buy price also called "Bid" at 1.6490. The difference between the sell and buy price is called a SPREAD, therefore in our example the spread for GBP/USD is approximately 7 pips. Once you execute a trade, spread is the only cost which you have to bear as most of the Forex brokers do not charge a commission. Spread is a way by which the brokers receive their revenue. Majority of the currency pairs have a spread between 2-9 pips, but the average daily movement of these pairs is over 100 pips therefore you should not be overly concerned with a small spread. Certain brokers offer fixed spreads while some will have varied spreads and will increase the spread during holidays or turbulent market condition. The investor has to overcome this spread in order to make profit.

We assume that the financial uncertainties in England will have a negative impact on the Pound, therefore we are going to short the GBP/USD pair. From the example above we sold the Pound at 1.6483 and entered the trade at 5:00 p.m. Let's see what happens with our GBP/USD trade. At 8:10 pm the trade has moved in our direction and we close the trade by buying back the Pound at 1.6479, therefore making a profit of 4 pips.

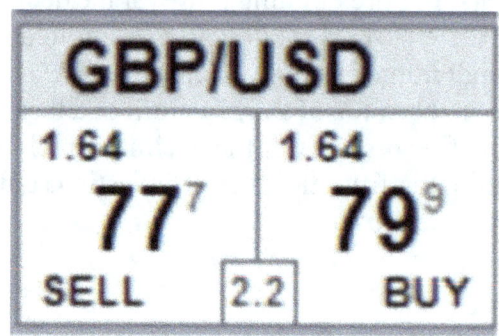

Please note that for simplicity sake we are not considering the 5th digit after the decimal. If we take the 5th digit in consideration then we would have gained 3.5 pips .In this example above you also would have noticed the "variable spread" in play. When we sold the pair initially the spread was approximately 7 pips and later on when we bought back the pair the spread had changed to 2 pips. If the spread would have stayed constant at 2 pips then we would have profited 9 pips instead of 4 pips we netted.

Please review the USD/JPY pair below and see how confidently you can answer the following question:

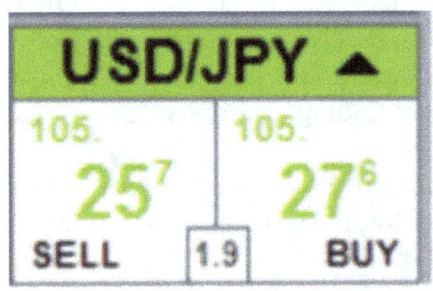

1. What is the current spread for the USD/JPY pair where sell price is 105.25 & the buy price is 105.27. Note; Yen pairs have only 2 digits following the decimal.

    Answer: _____ pips

2. Due to continuous efforts on the part of Bank of Japan to weaken the yen, let's say we decided to buy USD/JPY at 105.27 at 4:46 PM today. Please state the following:

    a. which currency you bought = _____
    b. which currency you sold = _____

3. At 5:14 PM you see that the USD/JPY is trading at 105.34 and you decided to close your trade.

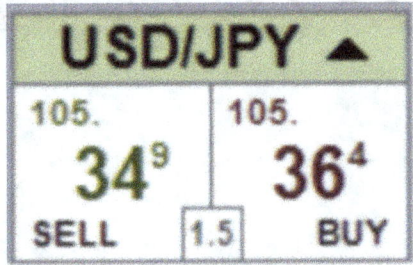

Upon closure of your trade:

   a. Did you profit or you suffered a loss = _____
   b. How much was the profit or loss = _____ pips

17

Disclaimer: The content on this page is for educational purposes only and should not be construed in any way as trading advice. The risk of loss in online trading of stocks, Forex, options, and foreign equities is substantial.

TRADING LOTS:

Currency pairs are traded in lots. When you buy one lot of EUR/USD, you purchase 100,000 units of that currency, where 1 pip is equal to $10. If your trade gains 5 pips then you would make $50 in profit, as each pip equals $10. A regular Forex trading account will allow you the ability to trade regular lots and you will be required to fund your trading account with reasonable amount of money.

For traders who are new to Forex and don't have the ability to start with a large amount, it is recommended that they open a Mini account and trade Mini-lots. With a mini-lot you purchase 10,000 units of a currency, where each pip equals $1.
Individuals who would like to start with an even smaller account and reduce the risk; micro accounts are available which gives you an opportunity to trade micro lots. One pip equals $0.10 for a micro-lot. There are Forex platforms that will allow you to trade smaller lots than micro lots. I would prefer a trading account where I will have the ability to trade any lot size based upon the funds I have in my account.

The general recommendation about the type of account you should operate is as follows:

CAPITAL	UNITS OF CURRENCY TRADED	VALUE PER PIP
$100.00	10 units	1/10th of a cent
$1,000.00	100 units	$0.01
$10,000.00	1000 units, micro-lot	$0.10
$100,000.00	10000 units, mini-lot	$1.00
$1,000,000.00	100000 units, lot	$10.00

Disclaimer: The content on this page is for educational purposes only and should not be construed in any way as trading advice. The risk of loss in online trading of stocks, Forex, options, and foreign equities is substantial.

Quiz Time:

4. You recently started trading live, after funding you Forex account with $ 10,000. You opened a trade by going long the NZD/USD pair using one micro-lot. The trade was entered on 11/16 at 0.8089. The trade moved in your direction and you exited the trade on 11/28 at 0.8243.

Please review the chart on the following page and answer the following questions:

   a. With $10,000, what type of account you would like to open?
      Answer: _____ account

   b. How many pips you gained when you closed the trade on 11/28?
      Answer: _____ pips

   c. What is your profit in dollars for this trade?
      Answer: _____ dollars

   d. The value of each pip for a micro-lot is
      Answer: _____ dollars

Disclaimer: The content on this page is for educational purposes only and should not be construed in any way as trading advice. The risk of loss in online trading of stocks, Forex, options, and foreign equities is substantial.

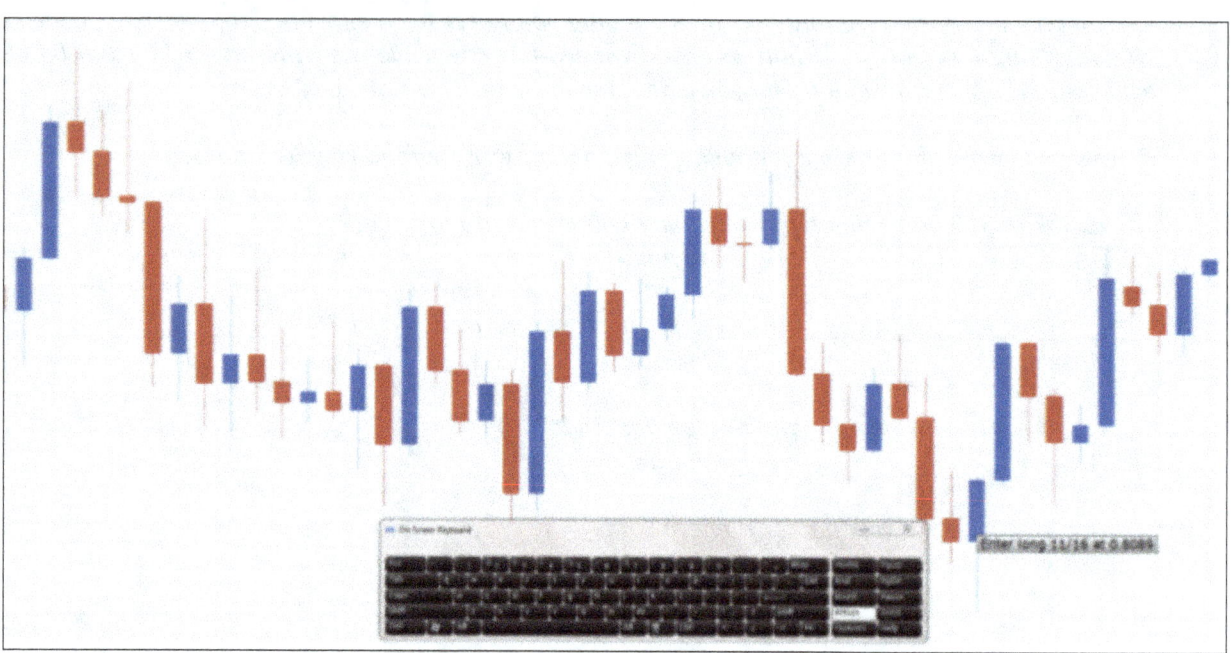

LEVERAGE AND MARGIN:

Forex is a leveraged market, what it means is that you are using a small amount of money in your account to control a large amount of money in the trade. The level of leverage allows the investor to either make huge sums of money or to lose a significant sum. Due to recent changes in regulations in the USA, the maximum leverage available to retail Forex investors is 50:1. In the UK the investors are able to trade Forex with a leverage of 100:1 to 200:1.

The current EUR/USD exchange rate is 1.2900; if you were to use 1:1 leverage then you have to pay 1.2900 dollars to buy 1 unit of euro. Let's assume that over the next 15 days EUR/USD appreciates to 1.3000, in trading terms that is a gain of 100 pips, and as you were not leveraged and you only bought one unit of euro, you stand to gain 1 cent. This scenario is not very exciting and it is not worth my time to chase that one cent profit. The use of leverage makes the above mentioned trade an exciting prospect with an opportunity to make larger profit. It is also important to remember that the risk of loss also rises proportionally once leverage comes into play.

With 50:1 leverage available you would have been able to purchase 50 units of euros with the same amount of money, for the above mentioned example thereby profiting 50 cents. Still not exciting, isn't it? I hear everybody saying too little profit! OK; then let me explain how this leverage plays out in a real trading account.

Type of Forex Account	Sum of money in the account	Leverage Used	Micro-lots allowed with this Leverage	Pair Traded	Buy on 11/17	Sell on 11/25	Profit in Pips	Profit in US dollars
MICRO	$10,000.00	1 to 1	10	NZD/USD	0.81	0.82	100	100*0.1*10 = $100
MICRO	$10,000.00	50 to 1	500	NZD/USD	0.81	0.82	100	100*0.1*500 = $5000
Therefore with same amount of money & time spent using 50:1 leverage allows a handsome profit on this trade							Difference	$4,900.00

Summary:

We will need 0.81 dollars to buy one unit of New Zealand Dollar (NZD)
One micro-lot is 1000 units therefore in order to buy 1000 units of NZD we need $ 810
We have a total of $10,000 in our account therefore we can safely buy is 10 micro-lots (10,000 units) with $8100. (Theoretically you can open 12 units which will require a margin of $9720, but for simplicity sake we are going to buy 10 units)

Here you can see that with 1:1 leverage you require at least $ 8100 set aside in your trading account.

If we are given a leverage of 50:1 then the equation will be as follows:
In order to buy one micro-lot of NZD (1000 units) with 50:1 leverage we only need $810/50 = $ 16.2
*Therefore we can purchase 500 micro-lots with $10,000 in our account. $16.2*500 = $8100*

Remember with a micro-lot each pip equals $0.10, therefore when we gain 100 pips, we make $100 as we were trading 10 micro-lots at 1:1 leverage. With 50:1 leverage we were able to open 500 micro-lots and once our trade made 100 pips we gained $5000.

The amount of money required to be set aside to open a trade is called margin. Majority of the trading stations will allow you to trade at 50:1 leverage. In the example above the margin required to open 500 micro-lots was $ 8100. The margin does not leave your account. If you close the trade with a profit of $100 as above, your account capital will gain $5000 and the account balance will be $15,000 at the end of the trade with the margin released.

If the same trade goes against you then there is a possibility of a margin call and your trade getting closed by your broker. Once you open 500 micro-lots of NZD/USD, $8100 is set aside that means you are left with $1900 free in your account. As long as your trade does not get negative by $1899 your account is OK, but as soon as the trade gets to negative – 1901 your trade will be liquidated and you will be left with only $ 1899 in your account. This highlights the risk associated with leverage trading and later on we will discuss that how much risk you should take while trading.

Quiz Time:

5. You operate a micro account and have $10,000 in trading funds. Your broker allows you 50:1 leverage. You are planning to enter long the AUD/USD at 1.04, with your knowledge of the basics of Forex trading please answer the following questions:

   a. *Theoretically how many micro-lots of AUD/USD can you buy* _____ *micro-lots*
   b. *What is the margin requirement for opening those lots* _____ *dollars*
   c. *If the trade goes against, at what negative value will your account receive a margin call* _____
   d. *If the trade gains 150 pips then what will be your profit in dollars* _____ *dollar*

Tough section isn't it, but if you are able to grasp these concepts then investing in Forex will be interesting. Take your time understanding these concepts, don't rush yourself. Let's take a break and we will meet shortly in a couple of hours.

FOREX CHARTS:

One of the important aspects of trading is the ability to interpret Forex charts. Trading where charts are the basis of trading is called "Technical Trading". There are Forex traders who spend hours upon hours as well as large sum of money mastering the charts and various indicators. In chapter six we will get into details of setting up your charts, but here I will introduce you to the various types of charts and the time frames these charts can be set up at.

There are charting packages which are available on the Internet free of charge and then there are packages which can cost you thousands. In addition almost all the brokers have some sort of charts incorporated or associated with their trading platforms. I personally will not spend any money on charting packages. Charts associated with your trading platform will suffice.

The charts can be viewed in various time frames, e.g. ticks, one minute, five minutes, hourly, daily, weekly and monthly. I am a big fan of hourly and daily charts. I do sometimes use weekly and monthly charts to review historical data. Some individuals are glued to their computers and trade off one and five minutes chart. I would never want to do that, but choice is yours.

The various types of charts are:

  a. <u>Line Charts:</u> It plots only the closing price and then the chart connects the closing prices with a single line. It provides limited information but provides a clean picture by removing the price *fluctuations seen during that time period. These charts have a role in clearly displaying patterns, for technical traders.*

    b.   <u>Bar Charts:</u> *These charts display more information than the line charts but are not commonly used by traders. I would not use them at all in my trading.*

    c.   <u>Candle Stick Charts:</u> *These are my favorite. The candles display the opening price, closing price, the low and the high for that time frame. The color of the body of the candle also tells us that the price moved up or down during that time frame. I will be referring to candle stick charts throughout this presentation.*

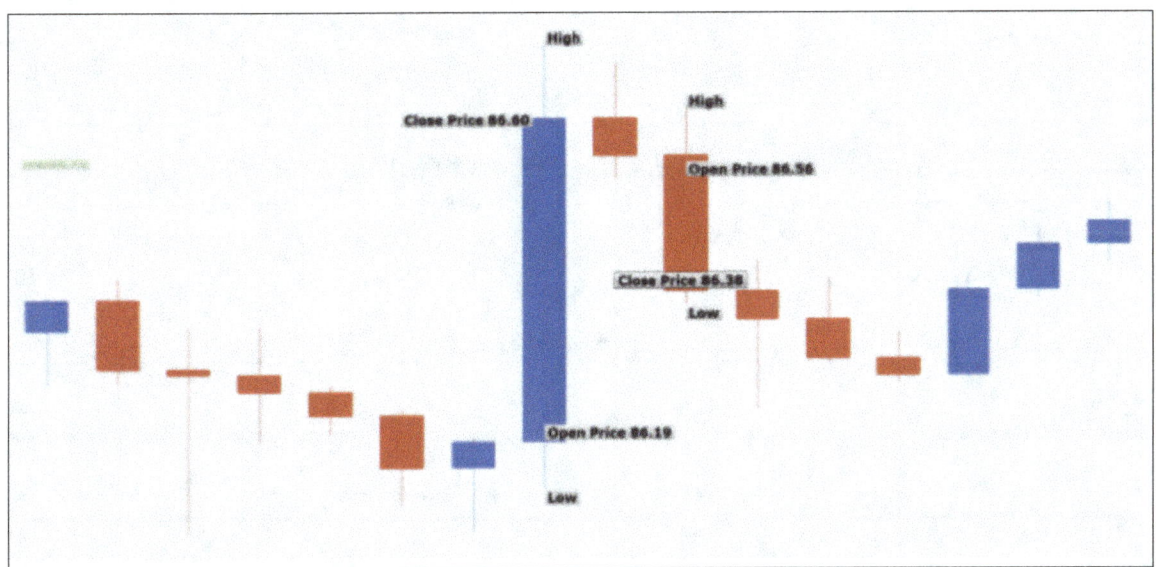

6. Above is an example of a zoomed in AUD/JPY hourly time frame Candle stick chart, where each candle represents one hour of price change. You should be able to count 16 candles therefore this chart displays last 16 hours of data for the AUD/JPY pair. The blue candles indicate price moving up and the red candles represent price moving downwards. If you went long the AUD/JPY pair at the open of the blue labeled candle at 86.19 and closed your trade at the close of the candle at 86.60 you would have netted 41 pips in one hour. What would be the outcome of your trade if you went long AUD/JPY pair at the open i.e. 86.56 of the red labeled candle and closed your trade at 86.38? What is your answer is it a positive trade or would it be a loss & by how much _____ pips?

Disclaimer: The content on this page is for educational purposes only and should not be construed in any way as trading advice. The risk of loss in online trading of stocks, Forex, options, and foreign equities is substantial.

Now let us see exactly the same hourly chart of AUD/JPY, as shown previously in the Bar chart form, as mentioned before I am not a fan of bar charts. Candlestick charts display the same Information in a much better format. Would you agree? Anyway the choice is yours.

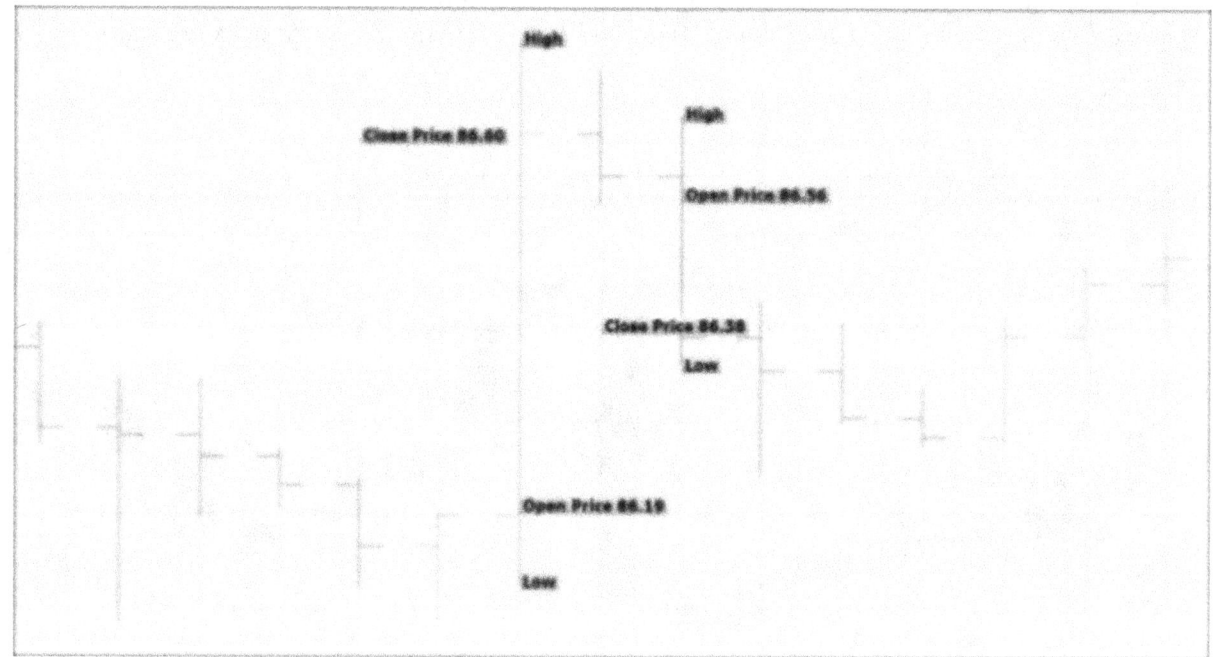

Now the same chart in the line format below:

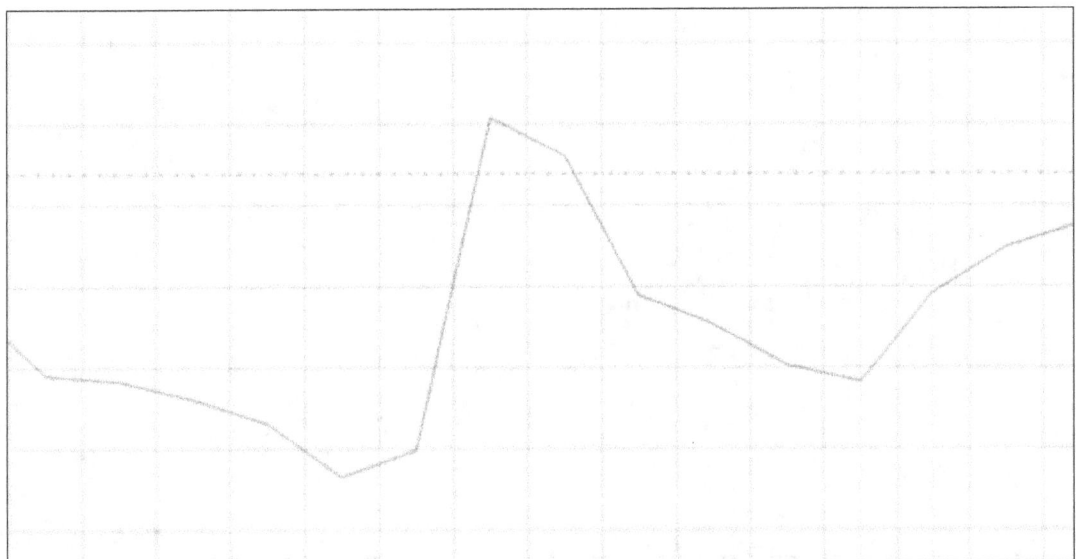

The chart above shows very limited information but has a role to play in technical trading.

Let me also share with you a zoomed out weekly chart for USD/JPY displaying the data for the last six years.

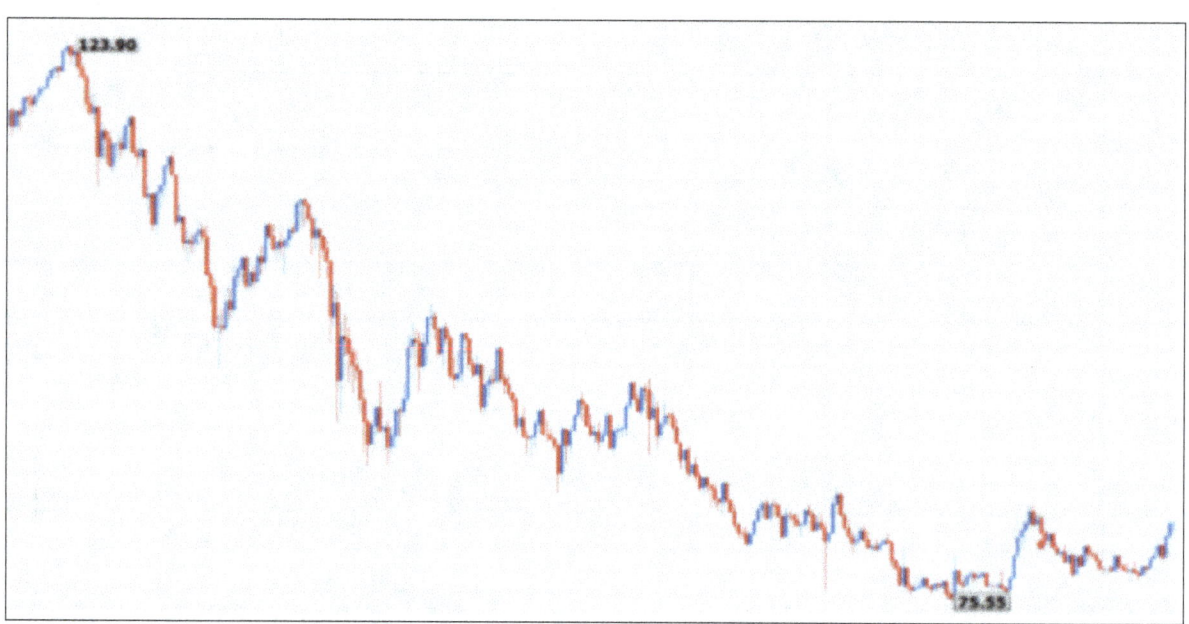

During a period of five years the price of USD/JPY has moved from a high of 123.90 to a low of 75.55.

It is time for me to take a break, as my wife is getting restless, she wants me at the dinner table; therefore, let me sneak in a final question for this chapter.

Imagine you had $10,000 in your trading account therefore you are able to trade 500 micro-lots. You opened the trade by selling the dollars and buying the Yen at 123.90. You kept this trade opened for the next 5 years and sold those yens when the price reached 75.55. How much profit would you have made from this trade? OK I will give you an answer, no need to calculate as you have been a patient audience. The profit for the trade was $2,417,500. Amazing right; Please take some time to digest these concepts described in this chapter. I will meet you tomorrow with a new chapter. Good night and happy reading.

FUNDAMENTALS IMPACTING CURRENCIES

CHAPTER FOUR

FUNDAMENTALS IMPACTING CURRENCIES

Good morning, I hope you are all rested and ready to learn about the fundamental factors that impact currency pairs. It is 8:00 am on a beautiful autumn Sunday morning here in Houston, Texas. The mellow rays of the early morning sun are filtering in through my bedroom window as I stroke the keys of my laptop along with intermittently sipping hot creamy coffee from my extra-large mug.

The factors impacting the value of a currency pair are driven by supply and demand principle. An increased demand of a nation's currency will lead to a higher value provided the supply of that currency does not increase at the same time. The supply and demand factors can be broken down into the following two categories:

    A. Trade Flow
    B. Flow of Capital

A. **TRADE FLOW:**

The economy with an increased production of goods which are in demand worldwide will have a positive trade flow and an appreciating currency as buyers are willing to exchange currencies to pay for those goods. Trade flow is affected by the following factors:

   1. <u>Balance of Trade:</u>   It is based on factors that impact the balance of imports and exports for any given economy. If the USA has to import goods from the European Union (EU) then it has to make the payments for these imports in euros, therefore they will sell the dollars and buy the euros for this transaction. As these transactions are in billions of dollars the price of the euro will increase. Conversely when the European countries import goods from United States they exchange their euros for dollars to pay for these goods. If the US imports from the EU exceeds their exports to EU then the US is said to carry a trade deficit with EU. More trade will flow towards EU rather than US therefore, Euro will gain strength.

   2. <u>Gross Domestic Product (GDP):</u>   The GDP represents total domestic economic growth. An increase in GDP means that the production in that country is rising due to demands from local or international buyers. This boosts the local currency as the goods and services have to be purchased in local currency. In the USA the GDP numbers are released on a quarterly basis.

   3. <u>Manufacturing Indices:</u>   These indices measure manufacturing activity within an economy, which includes new orders for manufacturing, inventory levels, production, supplier deliveries and employment. The economy with an increasing manufacturing activity will see an appreciating currency. In USA the two indices used to measure manufacturing activity are Institute for Supply Management (ISM) report and Purchasing Manager's Index (PMI). These numbers are released on a monthly basis.

4. <u>Industrial Production:</u>   This is a measure of industrial products and services output. Rising industrial production indicates a strengthening economy and a stronger currency. This economic report is also released monthly.

B. **FLOW OF CAPITAL:**

It represents the investment money flowing in and out of an economy based on Interest rates, Investment yields and safety of assets. The flow of capital is impacted by the following factors:

1. <u>Interest Rates/Central Banks Meetings:</u>   Individual Central banks during their monthly meetings will determine what the interest rate will be for that economy based on the underlying factors. Any increase in the interest rate will drive the value of a currency up as the rate of return increases on the investment within that economy. Here in USA the Federal Open Market Committee (FOMC) also referred to as "the Fed" determines the federal funds rate (rate at which the banks borrow from the federal government) and the interest rates.

2. <u>Consumer Price Index (CPI):</u>   CPI is a measure of Inflation. It is determined by an average price of a common basket of consumer goods. A rising price indicates inflation and the central bank will attempt to control inflation by raising the interest rates therefore causing the respective currency to appreciate. The decline in prices of a basket of consumer goods leads to deflation and the central banks will be looking at reducing the interest rates which in turn will make the currency less attractive. This index is released monthly.

3. <u>Producer Price Index (PPI):</u>   PPI measures the amount domestic manufactures are being paid for their goods. An increasing number indicates rising inflation with increasing likeliness of rising interest rates.

4. <u>Consumer Confidence Reports:</u>   These reports are based upon a survey that asks the consumers of their optimism about the economy. If the consumers are confident about the growth of the economy they are likely to spend more which in turn will drive the value of the currency higher. In USA the important consumer confidence data is released by University of Michigan report.

5. <u>Labor Report:</u>   The labor report has two components, the unemployment rate and the number of non-farm jobs created for that month. This report is usually released on the first Friday of each month here in USA and results in significant movements in currency market. Generally lower employment rates indicate an improving economy and a stronger currency and vice versa.

Majority of the reports mentioned are released on a monthly basis. The calendar indicating the time of these releases is available on various free to access financial websites and various Forex forums. In addition some Forex platforms also have these releases incorporated within them. The calendars usually will indicate the last month figures as well as the estimates about the current numbers. These releases are categorized as high, medium and low impact releases based upon the effect on the movements in the currency markets.

Disclaimer: *The content on this page is for educational purposes only and should not be construed in any way as trading advice. The risk of loss in online trading of stocks, Forex, options, and foreign equities is substantial.*

A sample calendar is shown below.

Legend									
High Impact Expected			JPY	🟧	Tertiary Industry Activity m/m	📁	-0.1%	-0.3%	0.2%
Med Impact Expected			JPY	🟨	CGPI y/y		-0.9%	-0.9%	-1.0%
Low Impact Expected	Wed Dec 12	12:30am	AUD	🟥	RBA Gov Stevens Speaks	📁			
Non-Economic		3:00am	EUR	🟨	German Final CPI m/m	📁	-0.1%	-0.1%	-0.1%
Actual Pending		3:45am	EUR	🟨	French CPI m/m	📁	-0.2%	0.0%	0.2%
Related Stories		All Day	ALL	🟨	OPEC Meetings	📁			
FF Alert Inside		All Day	EUR	🟨	ECOFIN Meetings	📁			
Revision		5:30am	GBP	🟥	Claimant Count Change	📁	-3.0K	5.9K	6.0K
Up Next			GBP	🟥	Unemployment Rate	📁	7.8%	7.9%	7.8%
Green Number Better than forecast -or- revised better			GBP	🟨	Average Earnings Index 3m/y	📁	1.8%	1.9%	1.8%
Red Number Worse than forecast -or- revised worse		6:00am	CHF	🟨	ZEW Economic Expectations	📁	-15.5		-27.9
			EUR	🟨	Industrial Production m/m	📁	-1.4%	0.3%	-2.3%
m/m Month Over Month		6:45am	GBP	🟨	MPC Member Dale Speaks	📁			
q/q Quarter Over Quarter		9:30am	USD	🟨	Import Prices m/m	📁	-0.9%	-0.4%	0.3%
y/y Year Over Year		11:30am	USD	🟧	Crude Oil Inventories	📁	0.8M	-2.6M	-2.4M
K Thousand		12:30pm	USD	🟨	10-y Bond Auction	📁	1.65|3.0		1.68|2.6
M Million		1:30pm	USD	🟥	FOMC Statement	📁			
B Billion			USD	🟨	Federal Funds Rate	📁	<0.25%	<0.25%	<0.25%

Fundamentals do play a part in the long term trading but their impact on a day to day basis is debated by the traders. I personally would like to know the fundamentals governing various currencies but would not solely focus on them when making my investing decisions.

Immediately following the release of data there is increased volatility within the Forex market especially if the numbers are better or worse than expectations. Usually this volatility calms down minutes after the release. Some traders pay significant attention to the release of data and have trading systems designed around the release. They subscribe to expensive financial news feed channels who in most cases release data few seconds prior to the release to the public. The trades are entered and exited in those few seconds before the data is released to the public thereby taking advantage of this time lag and reaping significant profits. This is a dangerous practice and can lead to significant losses as the brokers widen the spreads during release time and you don't get the price as you desired to enter the market (slippage). You might also not be able to close your winning trade in this volatile market due to slippage and end by taking a huge loss. I am not a fan of news trading and will not recommend it, but I do consider fundamental factors while planning my future investments.

The fundamental factors are so intertwined that you might see a currency pair going south even when the release is positive for the currency. I would not even try to speculate why this happens as there are a lot of pundits who can fill columns writing about the reasons behind these moves. Do they believe in what they are writing, I prefer not to comment!

Disclaimer: The content on this page is for educational purposes only and should not be construed in any way as trading advice. The risk of loss in online trading of stocks, Forex, options, and foreign equities is substantial.

This brings us to the end of the first section of this book. There are thousands of articles and hundreds of books out in the market which discuss the basics and the fundamentals of trading, but if you are able to understand these preceding 22 pages and answer the questions within those sections then you are ready to proceed and take the first practical steps towards investing on your own. Please take your time in getting yourself acquainted to these concepts and read these pages one more time before you proceed. This book will be your companion and will hold your finger as you find your way through this astonishing and amazing world of Forex investing.

TECHNICAL TRADING

CHAPTER FIVE

TECHNICAL TRADING

Majority of Forex traders focus on technical analysis and spend time mastering the Forex charts. They look for trading opportunities by analyzing the price movements, trend lines, indicators, charting and candlestick patterns. Technicians develop systems based on indicators, trend lines and price patterns. These systems have set rules when to enter and when to exit the trade thereby eliminating ambiguity. Technical trading is a vast subject on which multiple volumes have been written. You will be amazed that a technical trader has more than 100 indicators available to them through their trading station and each indicator has multiple systems developed on it. Technical trading is based on past results and there is no guarantee that these systems will keep on yielding similar results in future, as the market is very dynamic and it keeps on changing. The experts in the field of technical trading are particular about the set-up of their charts; they draw trend lines, focus on support and resistance, pick their indicators exclusively and pay attention to price patterns, thus increasing the probability of a successful trade. In my opinion the market is so random that even a technical expert can have multiple losses on a trot. In this chapter I will introduce you to the concepts of Trend, Support and Resistance, Candlestick patterns, Indicators and Price patterns.

A. TREND:

At any given point the Forex market is either trending upwards (bullish), trending downwards (bearish), or moving sideways (channeling). Majority of the time the market is oscillating between a certain range, and the technical traders wait patiently for it to break the range, either to trend upwards or downwards, in order for them to get in the trade early on in the trend and profit handsomely. It is also important to note that the channeling market can also provide trading opportunities as shown in the charts on the following page. Trend can be identified visually or by the use of an indicator called a Moving Average.

1. <u>Visual identification of the Trend:</u> If the price action on the chart is moving from the lower left hand corner towards the upper right hand corner then the currency pair is said to be in a bullish trend, while the movement from the upper left hand corner to the lower right hand corner represents a bearish trend. Buying the currency pair in a bullish trend increases the likelihood of a successful trade and selling in a bearish trend will likely result in a profit. If the price action is contained within two price points then the pair is said to be channeling. The question of when to enter, when to exit and how much of capital to risk are taken into consideration by the technical traders when setting up their systems. We will look at some of the systems later on in the chapter.

Disclaimer: The content on this page is for educational purposes only and should not be construed in any way as trading advice. The risk of loss in online trading of stocks, Forex, options, and foreign equities is substantial.

EUR/USD Uptrend

Daily EUR/USD chart indicating uptrend. Price moved from 1.2741 on 11/16/2012 to 1.3216 on12/29/2012

A gain of 475 PIPS

USD/CHF Downtrend

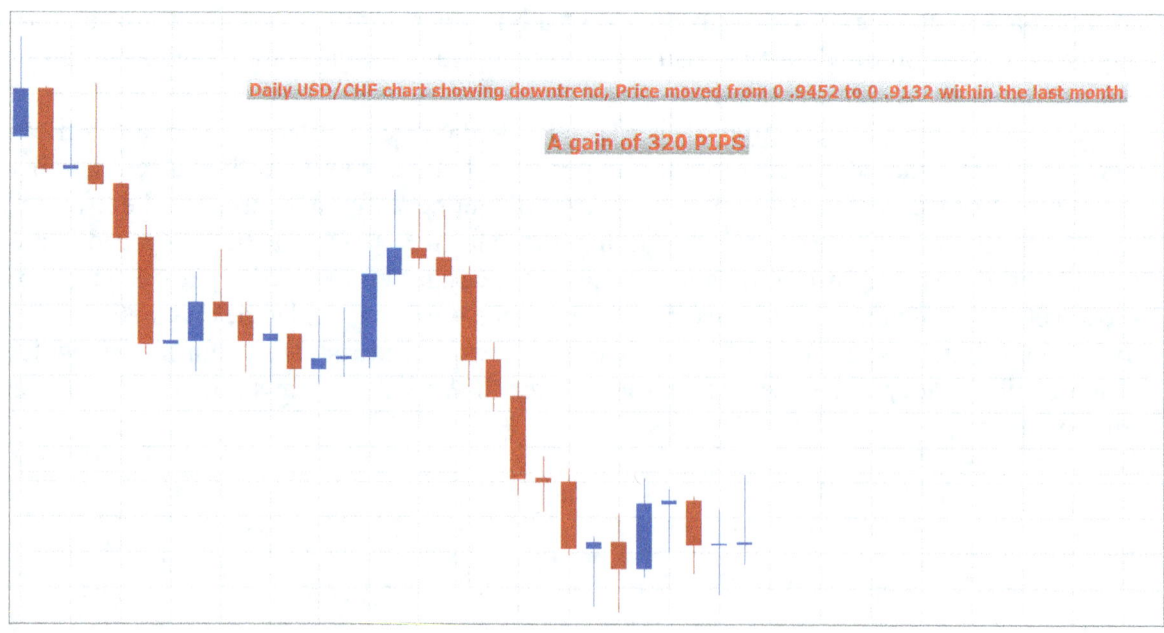

Daily USD/CHF chart showing downtrend. Price moved from 0 .9452 to 0 .9132 within the last month

A gain of 320 PIPS

Disclaimer: *The content on this page is for educational purposes only and should not be construed in any way as trading advice. The risk of loss in online trading of stocks, Forex, options, and foreign equities is substantial.*

GBP/NZD Channeling

Daily GBP/NZD chart, showing channeling from 9/14/2012 to 11/30/2012
Difficult to trade as the positions will be whip sawed on a regular basis

    a.   <u>Characteristics of an uptrend:</u>   As the currency pair moves upwards it creates a new high level following this new high the price retreats to create a lower level which is higher than the previous low and therefore is called a higher low. Upon resumption of an uptrend the price crosses the previous high to create a new high called a higher high & then retreats again. These series of formation of higher highs and higher lows characterize an uptrend and as long as these higher highs and higher lows are being created the uptrend stays intact. The formation of a new lower high or new lower low signals that the uptrend is getting weaker and it is time to lock your profits and exit the market and wait for a new trend to develop in order for us to get back in the trade. The periods of retraces during an uptrend allows us to add to our positions and/or adjust the stop levels for our trades in order to lock our profits. The daily chart of <u>EUR/USD</u> below, representing price action over the last one month, illustrates these characteristics. In addition the chart also highlights a simple system with set rules to follow in order for us to enter and manage a trade during this uptrend. Let us summarize the rules of this simple system:

* Once the trend starts, wait for the price to retrace
* Set your entry at 1 PIP above the previous high

* *Set your initial stop just below the recent low*
* *Let the new higher high and higher low to form*
* *Wait for price to break this new higher high*
* *Upon break of this new high bring your stop to 1 PIP below the latest higher low*
* *Keep on repeating these steps till the trend exhausts and your stop is hit and your trade closes*

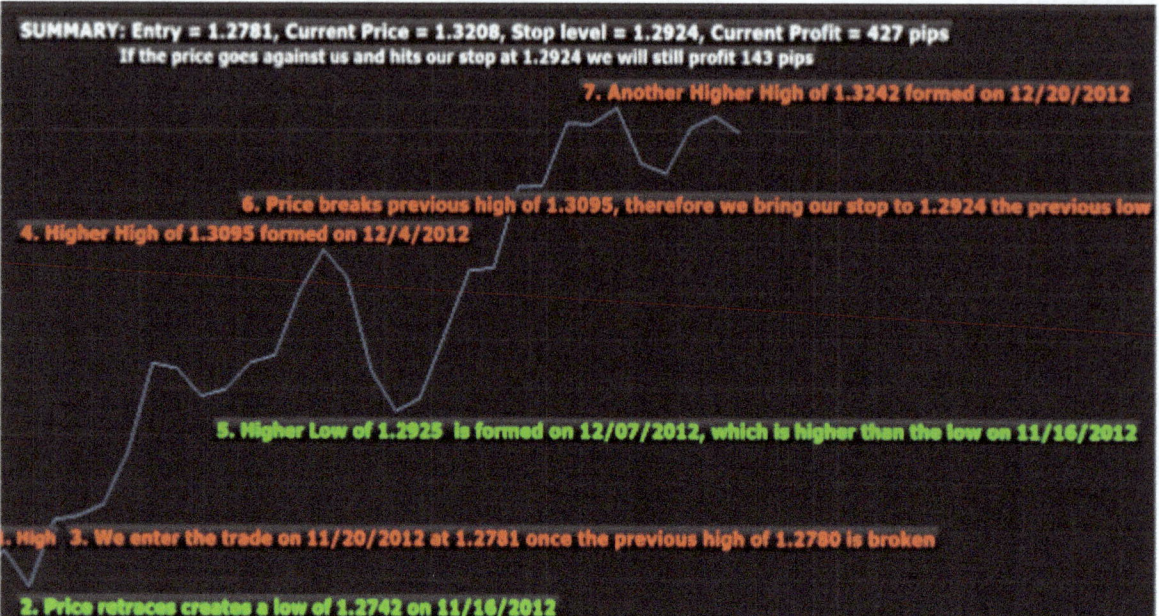

b. <u>Characteristics of a downtrend:</u> As the currency pair moves down it creates a new lower level following this new low the price retreats to create a higher level which is lower than the previous high and therefore is called a lower high. Upon resumption of a downtrend the price crosses the previous low to create a new low called a lower low & then retreats again. These series of formation of lower lows and lower highs characterize a downtrend and as long as these lower lows and lower highs are being created the downtrend stays intact. The formation of a new higher low or new higher high signals that the downtrend is getting weaker and it is time to lock your profits and exit the market and wait for a new trend to develop in order for us to get back in the trade. The periods of retraces during a downtrend allows us to add to our positions and/or adjust the stop levels for our trades in order to lock our profits. The daily chart of [USD/CHF](USD/CHF) below, representing price action over the last one month, illustrates these characteristics. In addition the chart also highlights a simple system with set rules to follow in order for us to enter and manage a trade during this downtrend. Let us summarize the rules of this simple system:

* Once the downtrend starts, wait for the price to retrace
* Set your entry at 1 PIP below the previous low
* Set your initial stop just above the recent high
* Let the new lower low and lower high to form
* Wait for price to break this new lower low
*Upon break of this new low bring your stop to 1 PIP above the latest lower high
* Keep on repeating these steps till the trend exhausts and your stop is hit and your trade closes

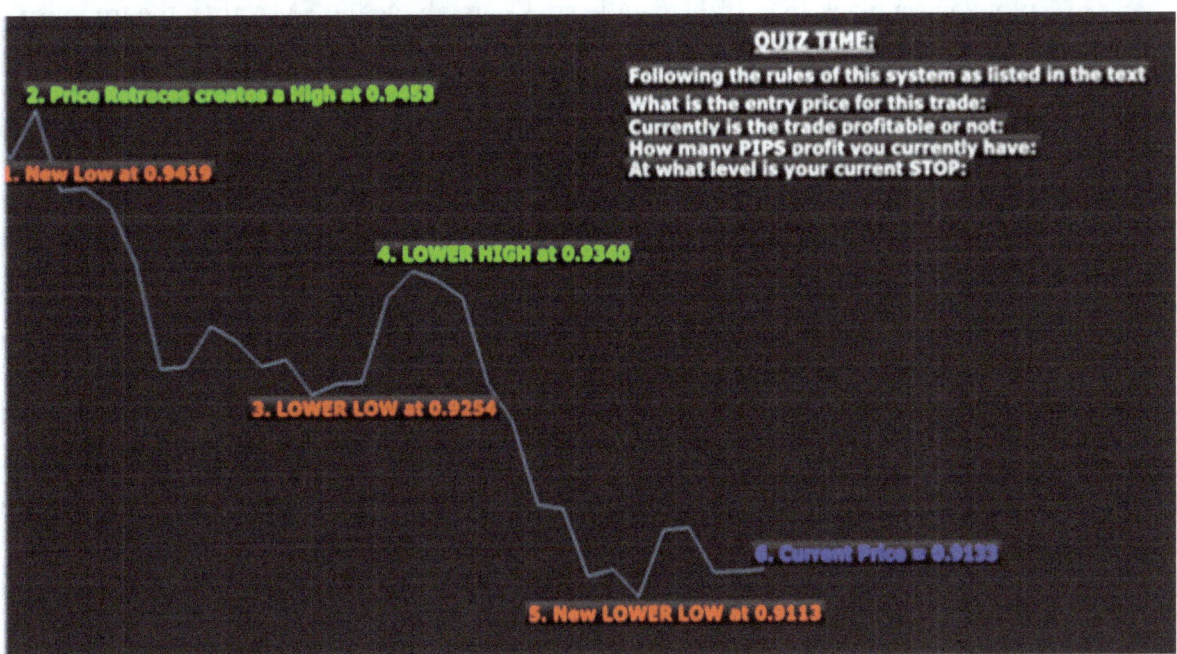

WORD OF CAUTION: It is important for us to know that even the professional and experienced technical traders find it difficult to accurately identify the start or an end of a trend. Actually their aim is to catch the middle part of the trend and increase the probability of a profitable trade as they trade along with the trend. There is no guarantee that once you enter the trade the price will move in a set pattern, the trend can immediately reverse on you and hit your initial stop therefore taking you out of the trade and leading to a loss. There is always a possibility that what you are seeing as a trend on one time frame is actually a retracement of an original trend on a higher time frame. Therefore I will recommend that if you are trading off a daily chart then you should at least review the weekly chart as well for that pair to see the original trend.

2. <u>Identification of the Trend by using a Moving Average:</u> The moving average represents an average of a closing price of an instrument taken over a certain period of time. There are multiple types of moving averages and for various time periods which are used by the currency traders. Here we are going to discuss the Simple Moving Average (SMA), and as we trade of a daily chart therefore I am going to use a 21 period SMA. This 21 period SMA takes an average of closing prices of a currency pair over the last 21 days and plots it graphically on the Forex chart. In simple terms on a daily basis the previous 21 days average is taken and plotted on the chart.

The reason we are using a 21 period moving average on the daily chart is because there are about 21 trading days in a month and this gives us a fair idea about the trend over the last month. As Moving averages are simple to read and use therefore it forms an integral part of Forex charts for a majority of traders. Some technicians use only a single moving average to determine a trend while others will use two to three moving averages and their cross over to determine the trend.

    a. <u>Use of a single SMA to determine the trend:</u> The daily chart on the following page of <u>USD/JPY</u> represents price action over the last 6 months. The chart has a 21 day SMA plotted as a black line. If the candle sticks are above the SMA then the trend is said to be bullish and traders will only take long trades or buy that particular currency pair. On the other hand if the price is below the SMA then the bear trend is in play and we will be selling the currency pair. If the price keeps on traversing the SMA on a regular basis then the pair is most probably channeling as shown on the chart. Let us create a simple system which will give us clear rules on when to enter and exit the trade using the SMA and look at the results of our system on the chart. Let us summarize the rules of this simple system for an up-trend:

* Let the candlestick cross from below the SMA to above the SMA
* Wait for another positive (blue) candlestick to form above the SMA. This candle should be a proper candle closing higher than the previous candle. This wait prevents you from entering into a false trend and getting whipsawed.
* After these candles form enter at the beginning of the next candlestick
* Exit once the candlestick closes below the 21 period SMA
* Set your initial stop below the recent low.
*Exactly reverse these steps for entry and exit for entering short in the downtrend.

As you can see from the chart above that when the price is channeling, a lot of false signals are generated leading to losses, it is only after # 15 when the market starts trending that we see good profits. It is important to note that there is no way of predicting with certainty that when the trend will begin therefore you have to be prepared to take small losses and position yourself to catch the big move which will allow you reasonable profit. In the chart above we see a gain of 302 pips over a six month period on one pair. The profit in dollars will be determined, based on your account and lot size. (Review TRADING LOT section in chapter 3)

Here we will take a little break this will allow you an opportunity to review this highly technical information and allows me time to check on my kid's homework.

b. <u>Use of a multiple SMA's to determine the trend:</u> A number of technical traders prefer using two to three SMA's to determine the trend. They will use the cross-over of the SMA's to enter and exit the trade. The most commonly used periods are a 50 and 200 day SMA's on a daily chart. Let us create a simple system which will give us clear rules on when to enter and exit the trade using the SMA crossover and look at the results of our system on the chart. Let us summarize the rules of this simple system for an up-trend:

Disclaimer: The content on this page is for educational purposes only and should not be construed in any way as trading advice. The risk of loss in online trading of stocks, Forex, options, and foreign equities is substantial.

* Wait for the 50 period SMA to cross above the 200 period SMA
* At the open of the next candle following the SMA cross enter long in the trade
* Exit once the 50 period SMA crosses below the 200 period SMA
* Set your initial stop below the recent low.
*Exactly reverse these steps for entry and exit for entering short in the downtrend.

As an example I am going to review the daily chart of NZD/JPY over the last one year with a 50 and 200 period moving averages. We will also look at the number of trading signals over the last one year and analyze the results.

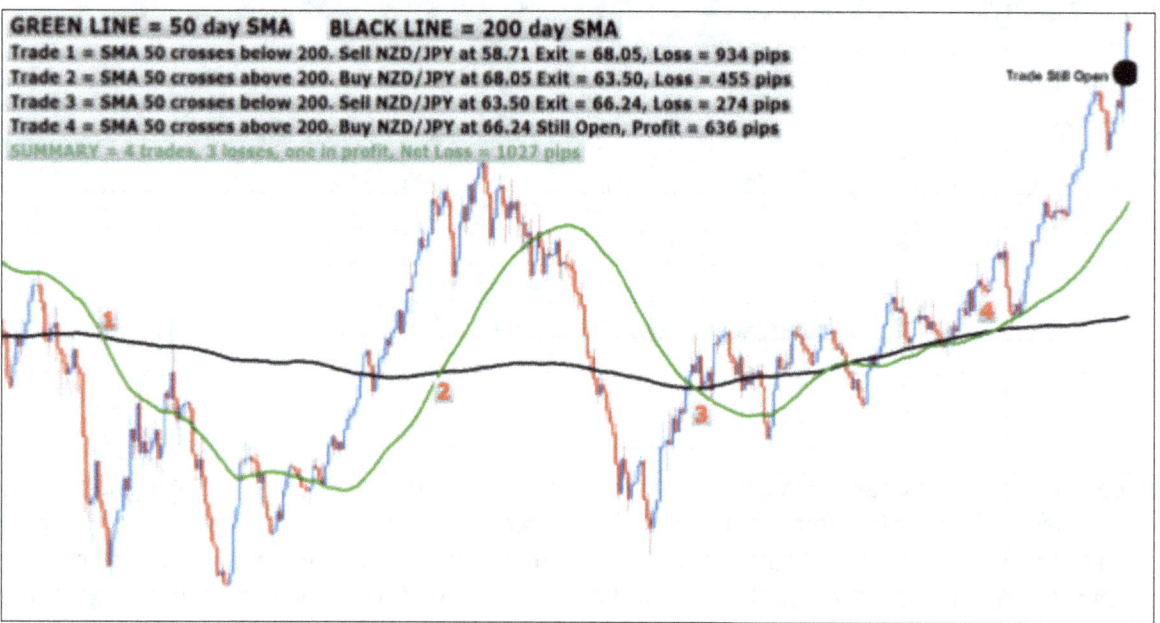

As you can see from the chart above that this SMA cross over system did not work well this past year, racking up a net loss of 1027 pips, as most of the JPY pairs were consolidating. Lately the upward trend has commenced and it may give us more positive trading opportunities on this pair in near future.

   B. SUPPORT AND RESISTANCE: Support and resistance are important areas on a chart which play significant role in technical trading. Technicians use these areas to enter, or exit trades and/or place stops and take profits for their active trades at these areas.

   1. Support: Support area is an imaginary price level on the chart that is difficult for the pair to break on the downside. The support line could be horizontal or oblique, and usually drawn as a green solid line on the charts by the traders. Ability to connect at least two or more price level with a line creates a valid support.

2. **Resistance:** Resistance area is an imaginary price level on the chart that is difficult for the pair to break on the upside. The resistance line could be horizontal or oblique, and usually drawn as a red solid line on the charts by the traders. Ability to connect at least two or more price level with a line creates a valid resistance.

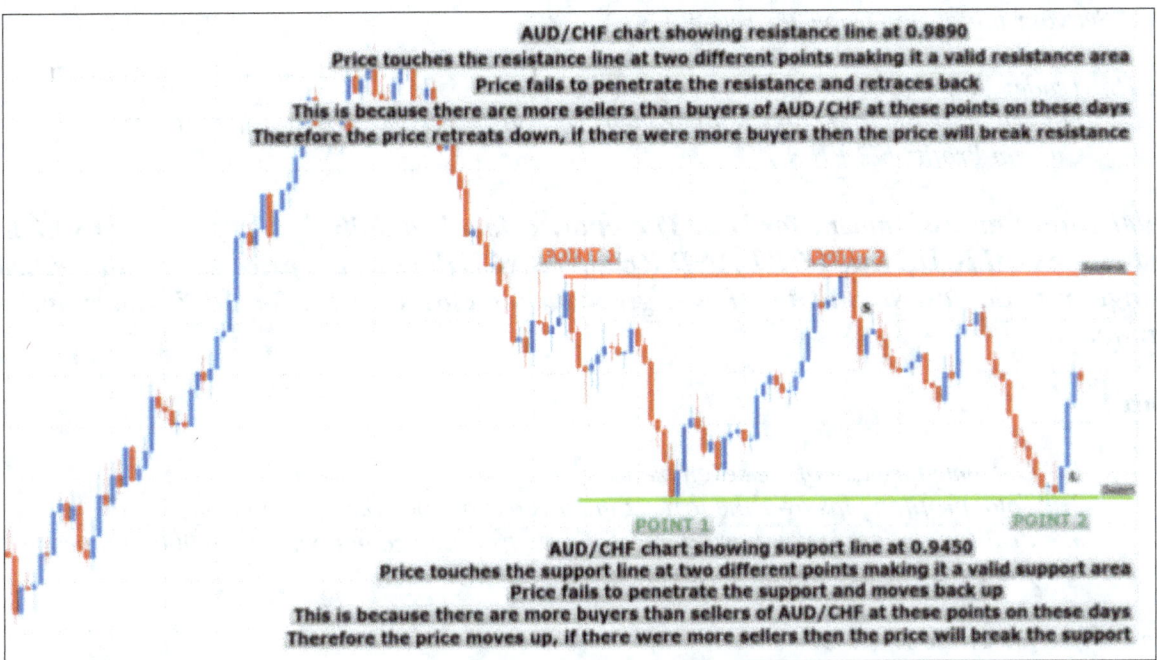

The above daily chart of AUD/CHF shows the price action settling in a nice 450 pips channel over the last 3-4 months, giving the technical traders opportunities at some good positive trades. Majority of technical traders will buy at support and sell at resistance.

Let us create a simple system utilizing the support and resistance line and see how can we enter and exit trades by following our rules. Summary of the rules for a short trades are:

* We will sell at resistance
* Wait for the price action to hit the resistance line and then form a good bearish candlestick.
* Enter short at the beginning of the very next candle. (Marked by "S" on the above chart
* Exit once the candlestick touches the support line
* Set your initial stop above the recent high.

RESULTS: Trade: Sell AUD/CHF at 0.9804 on 11/15/2012
              Close the trade at 0.9450 on 12/26/2012
              Profit: 354 PIPS

Summary of the rules for a long trade at support are:

* We will buy at support.
* Wait for the price action to hit the support line and then form a good bullish candlestick.
* Enter long at the beginning of the very next candle. (Marked by "L" on the above chart
* Exit once the candlestick touches the resistance line
* Set your initial stop below the recent low.

RESULTS: Trade: Buy AUD/CHF at 0.9512 on 1/02/2013
We will close the trade at 0.9890, trade is still open and the current price is 0.9682
Current Profit: 172 PIPS

As usual I have an assignment for you. The chart below is a daily GBP/CHF chart which clearly delineates the OBLIQUE SUPPORT AND RESISTANCE lines as the price action has settled within this range over the last six months. I will give you the closing price for all 7 trades and you will determine:

Quiz 1

1. Outcome for each of the seven trades
2. Total profit in pips over the last six months as you took these seven trades
3. Profit in dollars if you have a micro Forex trading account with $ 10,000 in your account and you were buying or selling 100 micro-lots for each trade.

Close Price for Trade 1: 1.4990
Close Price for Trade 2: 1.5246
Close Price for Trade 3: 1.4900
Close Price for Trade 4: 1.5138
Close Price for Trade 5 & 6: 1.4716
Current Price for Trade 7 as it is still open: 1.4848

It is important to note that sometimes the price will penetrate through the support and resistance leading the traders to enter the short or long trade respectively. Upon entering the trade the trade goes against the traders, reverses and enters back into the channel. The professional traders are ready for these scenarios they will take these losses and position themselves for another trade. In the GBP/CHF chart above a similar situation developed few days before we took the 4th trade and as we followed our rules we did not enter that false breakout.

With little practice you can become proficient in drawing these support and resistance lines on your Forex charts. Almost all the charting systems have drawing tools which can be used to draw horizontal or oblique lines with different colors and thickness.

How to trade a break of Support or Resistance Lines:

There are two simple ways a trader can trade a break of support or resistance. Commonly the traders will wait for the candle to either close below or above the support and resistance respectively. Then they wait for the price to come back and retest these lines and enter either short or long based on retest of support or resistance lines. The stop is placed around the midpoint of the channel and the profit target is equal to the width of the channel.

Disclaimer: The content on this page is for educational purposes only and should not be construed in any way as trading advice. The risk of loss in online trading of stocks, Forex, options, and foreign equities is substantial.

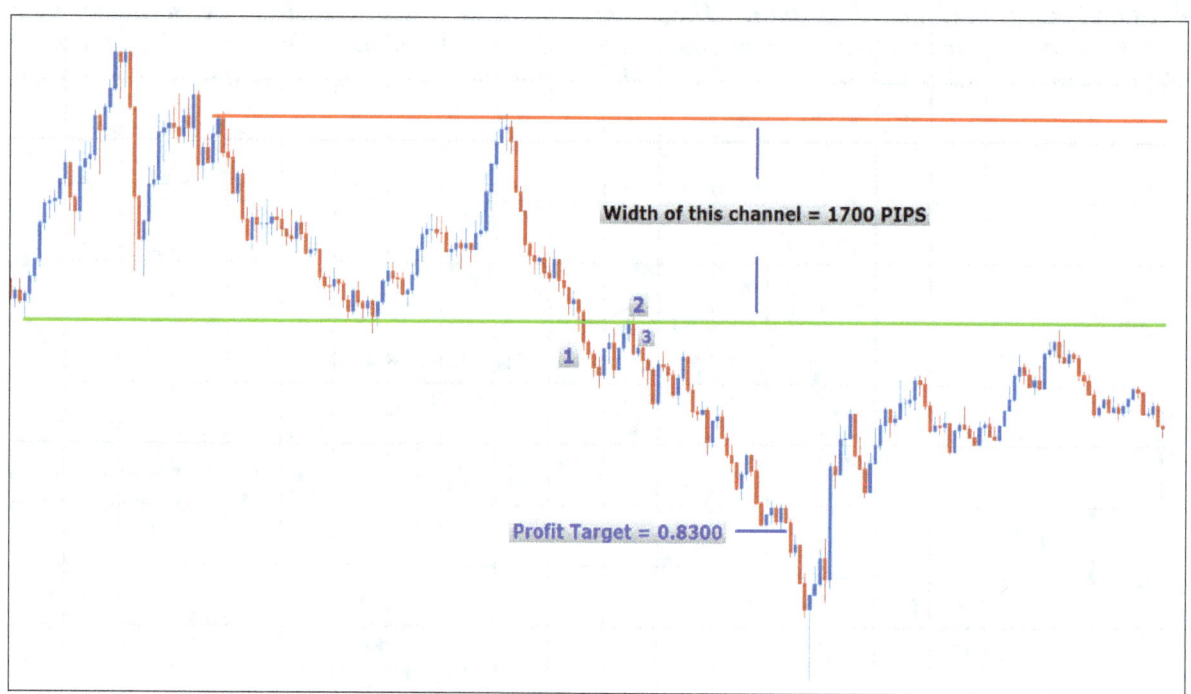

In the weekly USD/CHF chart above, which represents price action for the past five years, a nice support and resistance areas have formed. The width of this channel is about 1700 pips. The candlestick breaks the support (1) on 9/18/2012. Instead of immediately entering the traders wait for the price to retrace a little and retest the previous support in this case. The retest happens (2) on 11/20/2010. A nice bearish candle forms next week and we enter short at the start of the next candle after the bearish candle (3) at 0.9753. We place our stop somewhere in the middle of the channel at around 1.0800 and our profit target at around 0.8300, which is 1700 pips below the support line as 1700 pips, is the width of our channel. The trade plays out nicely and the profit target is reached on 06/25/2011, with a profit of 1453 pips.

Disclaimer: The content on this page is for educational purposes only and should not be construed in any way as trading advice. The risk of loss in online trading of stocks, Forex, options, and foreign equities is substantial.

Another way to trade the break of support or resistance is to have a predetermined entry level set below or above the support & resistance respectively. Once the price action breaks the channel and heads in the direction of your entry the trade gets triggered, upon entry into the trade the stop and take profit targets can be set. Usually the entry point is set at 10% of the width of the channel, below or above the support or resistance lines respectively. The take profit is equal to the width of the channel and the stop will be 10% of the width of the channel from the support or resistance line & is within the channel. In the USD/CHF chart below our short entry was executed at 0.9830 on 9/18/2010. The profit target and stop levels are shown in the chart. Once the short trade was entered upon break of the support we will remove the long entry and let our trade play out. Please note that this method of trading the break of support or resistance does not work well in the case of oblique support and resistance lines as they keep on moving down and the entry level will have to be adjusted accordingly on regular basis therefore let us not consider this second method for oblique lines.

Disclaimer: The content on this page is for educational purposes only and should not be construed in any way as trading advice. The risk of loss in online trading of stocks, Forex, options, and foreign equities is substantial.

3. <u>Fibonacci Retracements:</u> can be described as a series of support and resistance lines which are used by the traders once the trend has developed to determine whether a trend is likely to reverse or will it continue in its present direction. Fibonacci Retracements are based on a mathematical sequence which consists of a series of numbers, each of which is equal to the sum of the preceding two numbers in the sequence. This was discovered by Leonardo Fibonacci and the numbers in sequence are: 0, 1, 1, 2, 3, 5, 8, 13, 21, 34, and 55 and so on until infinity. *What should be our next number, can you guess? 34+55 = 89, therefore our next number in the sequence is 89.* Keep on adding your last two numbers and this will provide you with your next number in sequence.

Quiz 2

It is quiz time now, please tell me the next 2 numbers in this sequence after 89, ------------ & --------------.

Another interesting fact is that if we take a set of any 3 consecutive numbers from the sequence and divide the first number by the third number then we get a ratio close to 0.380 and if the second number is divided by the third number then a ratio close to 0.619 is obtained. These ratios can be rounded to 0.38 and 0.62 and are termed as "Golden ratio" or "Phi" because of their significance in trading. Ratios of 0.38 & 0.62 can be represented on the chart as Fibonacci lines at 38% and 62% of the latest move. Another line at 50% of the trend move between the 38% & 62% line is also drawn on the charts, e.g. if we choose 3, 5, 8 as the three consecutive numbers, and divide our first number (3) by the third number (8) i.e. 3/8, we get 0.38 as an answer, if we divide our second number (5) by the third number (8) i.e. 5/8 then our answer is 0.62. You pick your own three numbers and see for yourself what ratios you calculate.

Usually the price in either a recent up-trend or down-trend will retrace to 38% before resuming in the direction of the current trend. An older trend will retrace to the 50% or 62 % support or resistance line. Therefore traders use these levels to place stop levels and add to their positions. A break of 62% support or resistance line will signal a reversal in trend therefore traders will exit their current positions and enter trades in the direction of this new trend.

The Forex charts will have a Fibonacci retracement drawing tool. Click on the icon and then drag the cursor from the recent low to the high or from the recent high to the low in the up-trend and downtrend respectively. The 38%, 50%, & 62% levels of these moves will be represented on the charts by lines automatically. Some charts will also draw lines at the 25% and 75% levels. These two levels are not significant levels but are used by some traders to reduce the risk for their trades by placing stops at these levels.

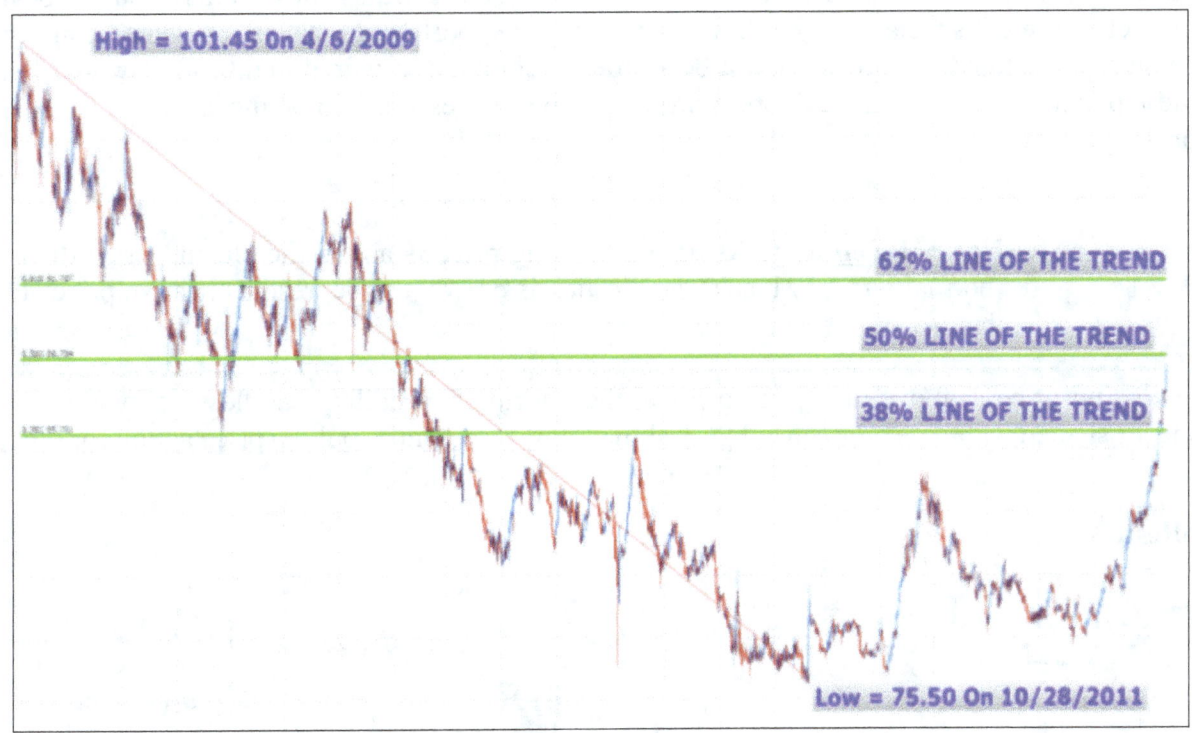

In the daily USD/JPY chart above, which represents price action for the past three years, a downtrend has formed. We take the high at 101.45 and a low at 75.50 and draw a Fibonacci retracement. The three retracement levels at 38, 50 and 62% are represented by the green resistance lines. Lately you can see the price retracing back to the 50% line. If the price continues to retrace back and breaks the 62 % resistance line then this current downtrend is over. The traders who are short this pair will exit and start looking for long trades. On the other hand if the price action stalls at 62% line and starts moving back down again then this trend is intact and the traders would like to add to their short positions for this pair.

Fibonacci retracement is an important tool in the arsenal of the technical traders and in fact multiple books have been written on the use and effectiveness of Fibonacci retracements. My philosophy on the use of Fibonacci and other indicators differs from the majority of traders which I will be explaining in detail in the following chapters. Here I would just like to warn that like all other technical indicators Fibonacci retracements can also generate a lot of false signals.

C. **CANDLESTICK PATTERNS:** Majority of Forex traders use candlestick charts. Candlestick charts can be set at various time frames ranging from one minute to monthly frames. Each individual candle on a chart displays the price action for that period. It outlines the open price, close price, the high and the low price reached during that time frame. By just looking at the candle the trader is able to determine whether the price action was bullish or bearish for that specific time frame. Traders also use various candlestick patterns to judge the sentiment in the market and look at specific areas on the chart where there is indecision between the bulls and the bears. These patterns have a bearing on market sentiment specially when they appear at the support or resistance levels and can point to a change in the trend. The patterns can be simple or complex, it is important to be aware of some of these patterns especially if they appear around support or resistance or at the extremes of an up-trend or down-trend.

1. **Normal Candlesticks**: If the opening price is above the closing price then a filled (normally red, or black) candlestick is drawn, this represents bearish price action for that period.

If the closing price is above the opening price, then normally a hollow candlestick (white with black outline, or shaded with blue or green color) is shown, this represents a bullish price action for that period.

Candlesticks

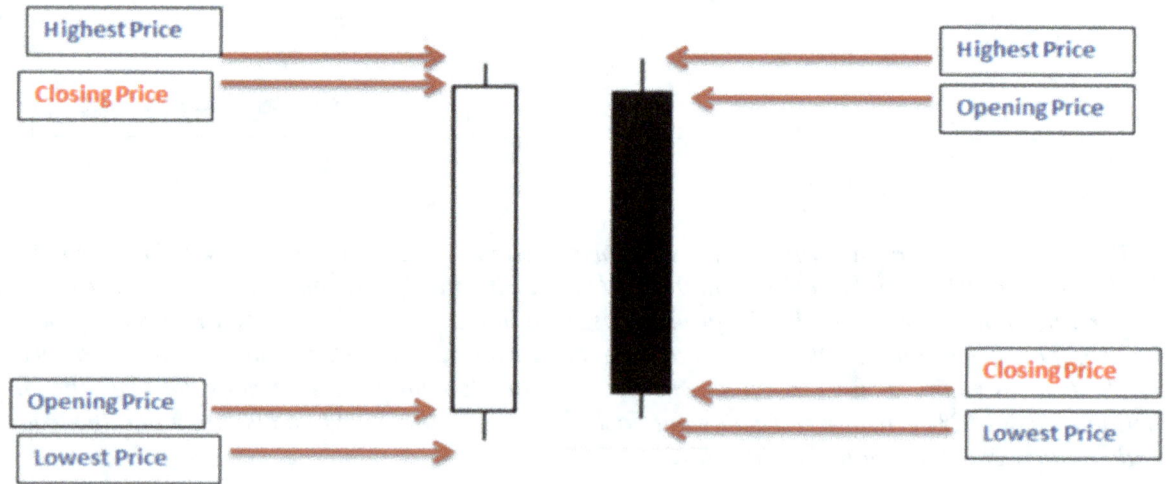

The body of the candlestick is filled if the closing price is below the opening price.

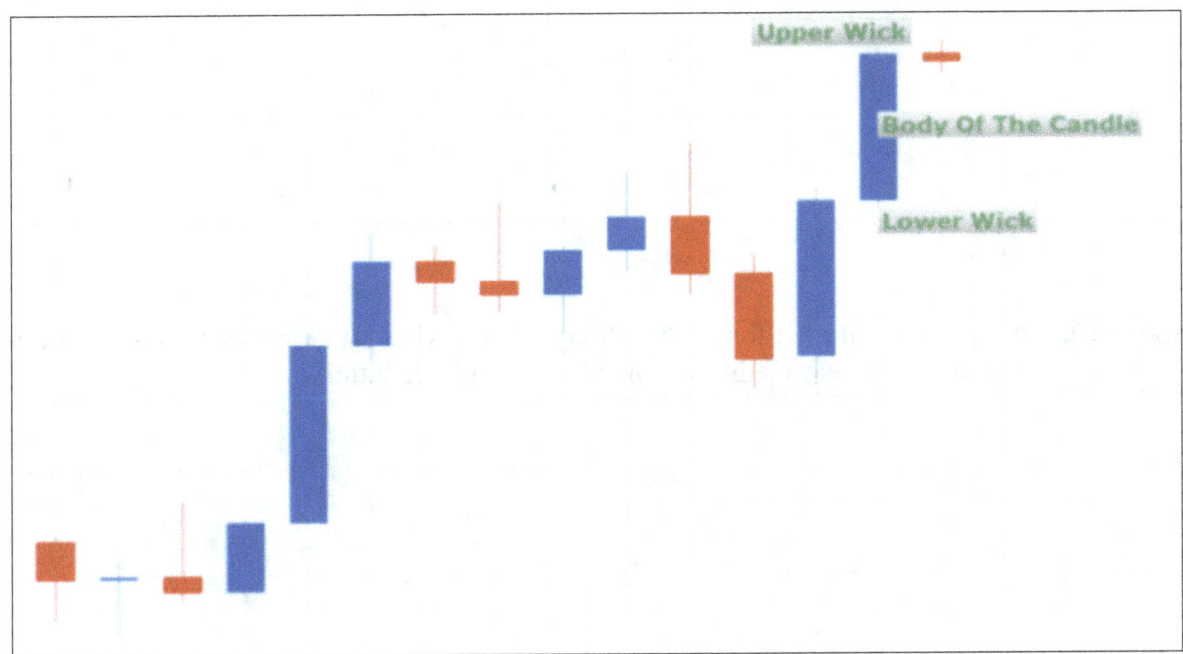

Quiz Time:

Quiz 3: In the example above which candle represents the price moving in an upward direction?

_____

2. **Simple Candlestick Patterns:**

This candle above represents quite a long black body with a wide range between high and low. Price opens near the high and closes near the low. Considered a bearish pattern

The above candle represents quite a long white body with a wide range between high and low. Price opens near the low and closes near the high. Considered a bullish pattern

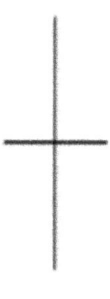

Doji

Doji forms when opening and closing prices are nearly the same. The lengths of shadows can vary; this pattern indicates indecision within the market.

Dragonfly Doji

Dragonfly Doji is formed when the opening and the closing prices are at the highest of the day. If it has a longer lower shadow it signals a more bullish trend. When appearing at market bottoms it is considered to be a reversal signal.

Gravestone Doji

Gravestone Doji is formed when the opening and closing prices are at the lowest of the day. If it has a longer upper shadow it signals a bearish trend. When it appears at market top it is considered a reversal signal.

Hammer

A Hammer is a black or a white candlestick that consists of a small body near the high with a little or no upper shadow and a long lower tail. This is considered a bullish pattern during a downtrend.

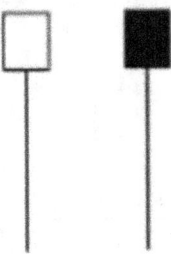

Hanging Man

A Hanging Man is a black or a white candlestick that consists of a small body near the high with a little or no upper shadow and a long lower tail. The lower tail should be two or three times the height of the body. Considered a bearish pattern during an up-trend.

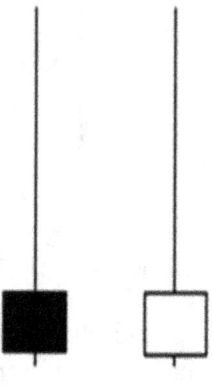

Shooting Star

A Shooting Star is a black or a white candlestick that has a small body, a long upper shadow and a little or no lower tail. Considered a bearish pattern in an up-trend.

3. **Complex Candlestick Patterns:**

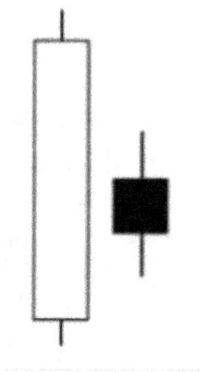

Bearish Harami

Bearish Harami consists of an unusually large white body followed by a small back body (contained within large white body). It is considered as a bearish pattern when preceded by an up-trend.

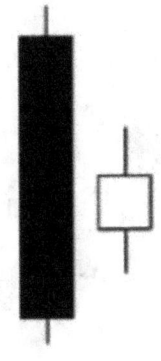

Bullish Harami

Bullish Harami consists of an unusually large black body followed by a small white body (contained within large black body). It is considered as a bullish pattern when preceded by a downtrend.

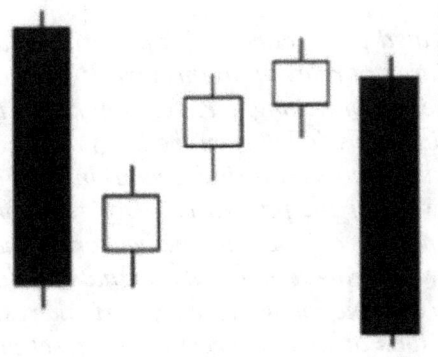

Bearish Three Method Formation

Bearish Three Method Formation has a long black body followed by three small bodies (normally white) and a long black body. The three white bodies are contained within the range of first black body. This is considered as a bearish continuation pattern.

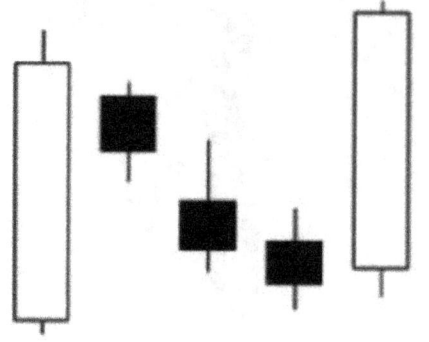

Bullish Three Method Formation

Bullish Three Method Formation consists of a long white body followed by three small bodies (normally black) and a long white body. The three black bodies are contained within the range of first white body. This is considered as a bullish continuation pattern

Word of Caution: *I have just illustrated a few candlestick patterns, and there are a lot more patterns which might have academic importance but are not relevant to this text. It is a good idea to be aware of these patterns but I would not use them solely for entering or exiting a trade. Majority of these candlestick patterns develop due to indecision in the market, representing a tussle between the bulls and the bears, therefore at any given time in a market there is either a bullish/bearish sentiment or indecision. Instead of focusing too much on the shapes of candlesticks and trying to determine whether the pattern is a Doji, dragonfly Doji, spinning top, shooting star, hammer or a Harami, I consider all as periods of indecision in the market and try to adjust my trades appropriately. On their own candlestick patterns may generate a lot of false signals leading to a potential losing trade. If these patterns interest you then using them in conjunction with the support and resistance levels will improve the chances of a profitable trade. We are going to look at some interesting trade set ups using the support, resistance levels and some candlestick patterns.*

The chart below is a GBP/USD daily chart representing price action over the last one year, during this time frame a nice support and resistance levels have formed at **1.5320** & **1.6260** respectively and the price action seems to be bouncing and retreating from these levels repeatedly. As the price action approaches support and resistance levels there seems to be indecision in the market, well-illustrated by Doji, shooting stars, etc. following which the price turns around. If we are in a long trade and as the price reaches the resistance levels and indecision seem to start becoming evident we book our profits and exit our long trade.

Here we wait for the price to turn around so that we can now enter a short trade and let the trade continue towards support this time. As the price action oscillated between support and resistance we had an opportunity to successfully execute three trades and also currently have two open short trades, which will be closed successfully once the price reaches the support level. In case the price turns around and pierces the resistance then we have safe stops in place just above the wicks of the candles at resistance, which will allow us to exit the trades with a smaller loss.

Disclaimer: The content on this page is for educational purposes only and should not be construed in any way as trading advice. The risk of loss in online trading of stocks, Forex, options, and foreign equities is substantial.

D. INDICATORS:

Forex traders seem to be fixated with indicators; their charts are loaded with these indicators to an extent that it is sometimes hard to separate a Forex chart from a piece of abstract art. These indicators range from a simple moving average to the fancy Ichimoku cloud or a McGinley Dynamic Indicator. Each charting package is inclusive of indicators where traders have the ability to select the time frame and variants of an indicator and plot it on their charts. My trading charts come with over 50 indicators. You will be amazed to learn that each indicator has a trading system based on it, and if you count the number of combinations these indicators can generate and the number of systems available, the value of these indicators is put into perspective. The sheer number of indicators and the trading systems related to them speak of how ineffective these systems can be over a long period of time as the market is dynamic, does not obey rules and keeps on changing. Moreover all these indicators are lagging in nature and will show the results after the price has already moved. The commonly used indicators are:

Moving Averages, simple, exponential or weighted,
MACD (Moving Average Convergence Divergence)
Stochastics (fast and slow)
Commodity Chanel Index (CCI)
Relative Strength Index (RSI)
Bollinger Bands

Ichimoku Kinko Hyo
Pivot Points
Average True Range (ATR)
Average Directional Index (ADX)
Elliot Wave Oscillator
and many, many more…

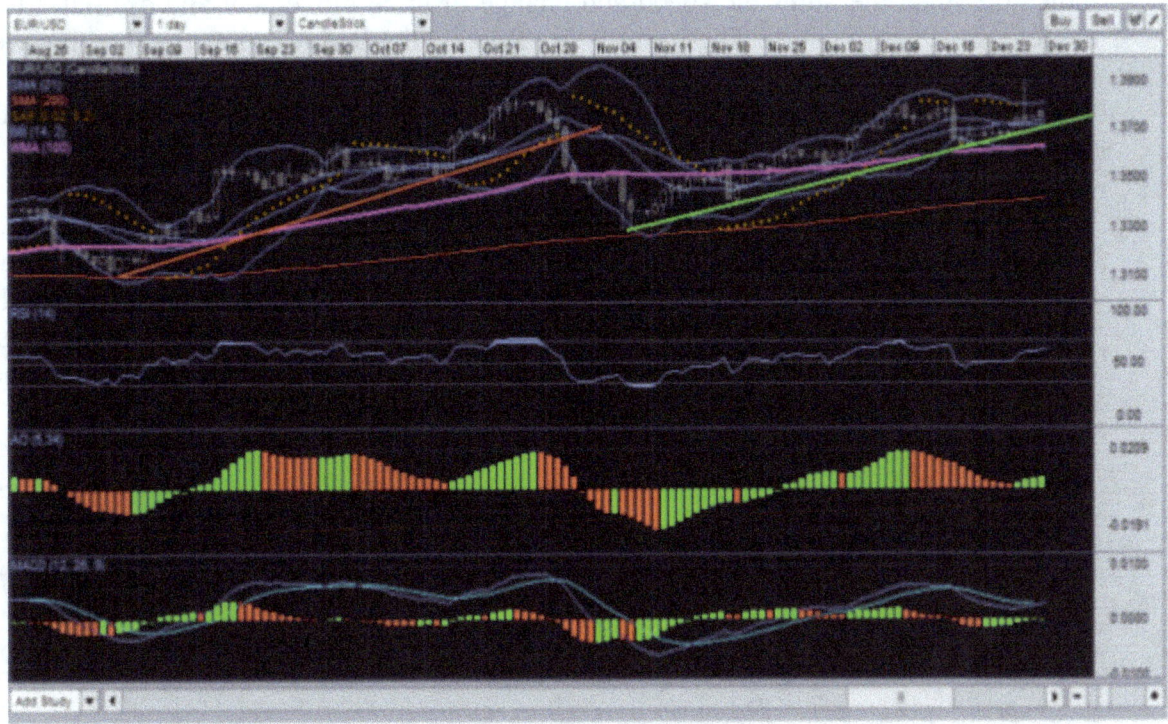

Above you can see a EUR/USD chart plotted with a few indicators. My personal preference is to set my charts without much of this clutter.

In-spite of all the drawbacks mentioned above regarding these indicators, majority of the traders have a few favorite indicators which they use frequently in Forex trading. They have systems developed on each of these indicators with well-defined rules, which are followed to the hilt. The traders do claim success with the use of the systems based on these indicators. Some traders are so confident that they will market signals for a fee to the community of traders to follow.

I am going to confess, that I also do have a soft corner for an indicator called Relative Strength Index (RSI). I do keep an eye on this indicator but won't trade the signals regularly but when I do take cue from the RSI I do it in a very peculiar manner. In the following paragraphs I will talk about the RSI, look at a system based on RSI and give you an insight about my way of trading with RSI.

1. <u>Relative Strength Indicator:</u> RSI was developed by J. Welles Wilder. It is a momentum indicator which measures the speed and change of price movement and oscillates between the levels of zero and 100. The formula to calculate the RSI is quite complex, but we don't have to worry about it as it is automatically plotted on the Forex charts once selected. From the list of indicators on your Forex chart, select RSI then select the time period and click apply and the RSI will be plotted in a separate window at the bottom of your chart.

The commonly used period for RSI is "14" on a daily chart. The currency pair is said to be overbought if the RSI level reaches above 70 & is oversold if the RSI is below 30. The levels allow the traders to short the currency pair when the pair is overbought and to buy the pair that is oversold. Here we develop a simple system based on RSI, define rules and see the results we achieved if we would have used that system on currency pair over the last one year.

Short (Sell) Trade:

* *Wait for the RSI to reach a level above 70*
* *Once the RSI closes above 70, we open a short trade on the pair at the open of next trading candle*
* *Exit the trade once the profit target of + 100 is achieved*
* *Place a protective stop at -50 pips from the opening price and the take profit level at +100 level from the opening price. This gives us a risk to reward ratio of 1:2*

Long (Buy) Trade:

* *Wait for the RSI to reach a level below 30*
* *Once the RSI closes below 30, we open a long trade on the pair at the open of next trading period*
* *Exit the trade once the profit target of + 100 is achieved*
* *Place a protective stop at -50 pips from the opening price and the take profit level at +100 level from the opening price. This gives us a risk to reward ratio of 1:2*

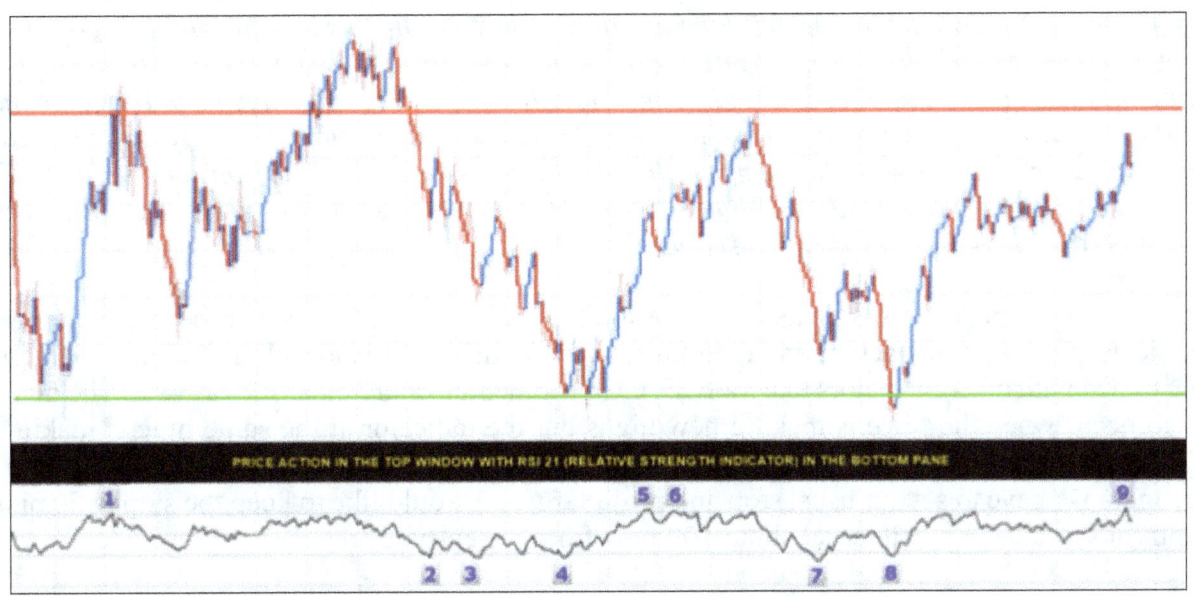

The chart above is a daily AUD/CAD chart representing price action over the last one year. The numbers in the RSI window of the chart represent the trades taken during the year. The summary of these trades is as follows:

Serial No.	Buy/Sell	RSI	Entry level	Stop level	Profit level	Profit/Loss in Pips
1.	Sell	71.33	1.0598	1.0648	1.0498	Hit Profit +100 pips
2.	Buy	26.64	1.0370	1.0320	1.0440	Hit Profit +100 pips
3.	Buy	27.19	1.0234	1.0184	1.0334	Hit Loss -50 pips
4.	Buy	27.59	1.0012	0.9962	1.0112	Hit Profit +100 pips
5.	Sell	71.98	1.0365	1.0415	1.0265	Hit Loss -50 pips
6.	Sell	70.88	1.0418	1.0468	1.0318	Hit Profit +100 pips
7.	Buy	27.65	1.0173	1.0123	1.0273	Hit Loss -50 pips
8.	Buy	26.92	0.9963	0.9913	1.0063	Hit Profit +100 pips
9.	Sell	72.70	1.0544	1.0594	1.0444	Open + 60 pips
Total:						Netprofit +560 pips

By following the rules of our RSI based system as defined on the chart above we entered nine trades during the last year for the AUD/CAD currency pair. Five of our trades were positive and three resulted in a loss while the ninth trade was positive at the time of writing. Overall we would have netted a profit of 560 pips using our system. Though our system was profitable last year but that does not guarantee success this year or the future years. The Forex market is so random that many successful systems can turn into losing systems over the next many years, therefore if anybody who claims to have an extremely successful mechanical system year after year, please take it with a grain of salt (except me of course, ha! ha! ha!). All the jokes aside I am going to discuss my investing methodologies in the last section of this book.

Disclaimer: The content on this page is for educational purposes only and should not be construed in any way as trading advice. The risk of loss in online trading of stocks, Forex, options, and foreign equities is substantial.

During a strong trend the system described above will fail miserably as the RSI and price can keep on climbing or falling in an uptrend or downtrend respectively. In these scenarios the pair can stay overbought or oversold for a long duration of time and the price does not reverse as it happens in a ranging market. You would have guessed by now that the AUD/CAD pair has been range bound over the last one year as the price keeps on oscillating between the support (green) and resistance (red) lines in the chart above. There was an attempt to break through resistance to the upside by the AUD/CAD pair between trade # 1 and trade # 2, but this break was not successful and the price action returned back within the range within a couple of weeks.

Instead of simply trading RSI signals once it reaches 70 or 30, I wait for divergence to develop between the indicator and the price action and then take the trade in the direction of an indicator. Divergences can be traded with other indicators like MACD, CCI, Momentum and Stochastics as well. The divergence is set to occur when the price is making new highs but the indicator at the same time is making lows, this indicates that the strength of the trend is weakening a bit and there is opportunity to take a contrarian trade, again we have to set our usual stop and profit targets. I would like to keep the stop at 50 pips from my entry level and the profit target about 100 pips from the entry level.

The chart below is a NZD/JPY daily chart, displaying the price action for the last one year. In the top pane the price action is visible while the lower pane displays the 14 period RSI. One thing I would like you to note is the strong trend NZD/JPY pair is currently in and the RSI is persistently and repeatedly staying above the 70 level. The RSI system rules listed above will fail because our trades will be stopped out with multiple -50 pip losses during this trend, therefore if the pair is trending I prefer to use the divergence method. Failure of the indicator to break the oblique resistance line (solid red line on the indicator in the charts below) at 3 attempts is a good sign that the time is ripe for us to enter a contrarian trade.

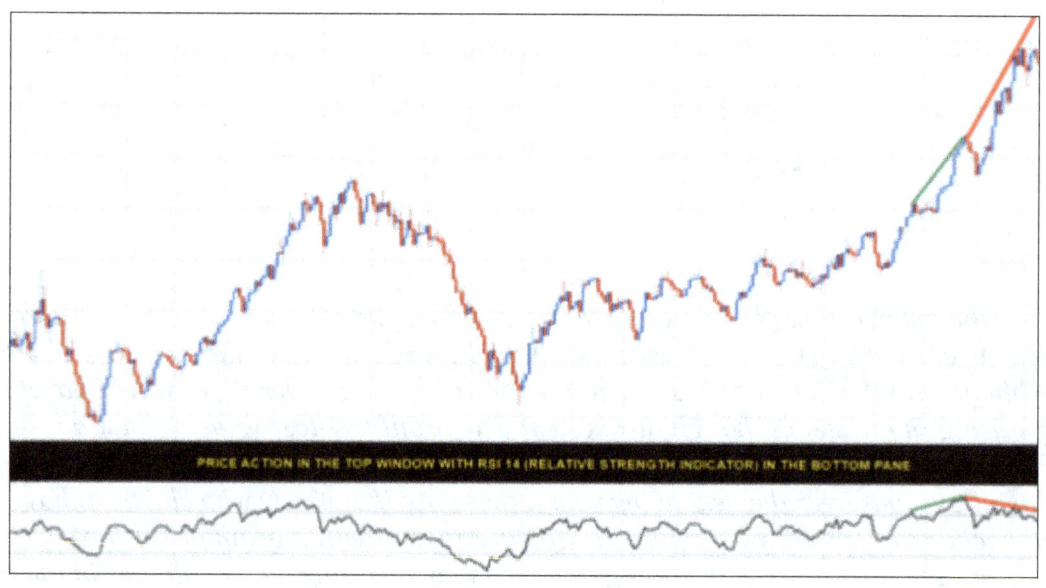

Disclaimer: *The content on this page is for educational purposes only and should not be construed in any way as trading advice. The risk of loss in online trading of stocks, Forex, options, and foreign equities is substantial.*

The chart above is of the NZD/JPY pair. Two solid green lines one on RSI and one on the price action and two solid red lines again one on RSI and the other one on the price action are visible. RSI reaches a level of 72, retraces a bit and then rises again to a level of 85. At the same time the NZD/JPY price reaches 68.00 then retraces a little followed by a new high of 71.00. The RSI level is rising and the price of the pair is rising at the same time indicating a strong up-trend (represented by green solid line) therefore I would refrain from taking a short contrarian trade.

After reaching the level of 85 the RSI has fallen back, it did cross above the 70 level again a couple of times but did not rise above the 77 level therefore making a low (represented by solid red line on RSI). But if you look at the price action at the same time the pair has reached a new high of 76.00 (represented by solid red line on the price action). This phenomenon is called divergence where the price is making new highs while at the same time the indicator (RSI in this case) is making lows. Here I can take a short (contrarian) trade and look for a 100 pip profit, still keeping a protective stop 50 pips above my entry level in case the trade goes against us.

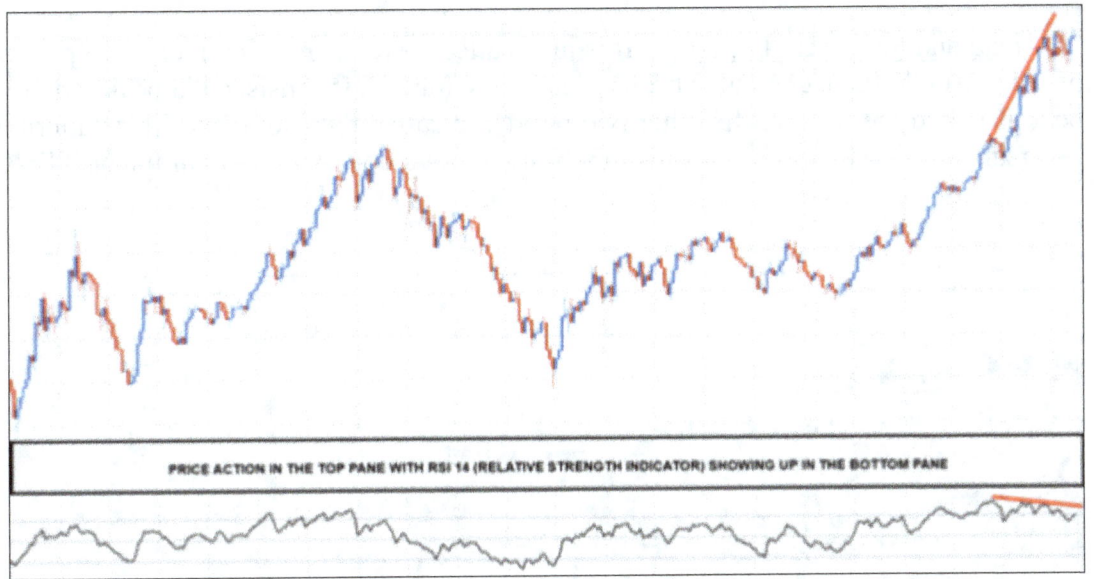

AUD/JPY chart above shows divergence between the indicator and the price action. AUD/JPY pair is making new highs (solid red line) while the RSI is making lows (solid red line)

E. **PRICE PATTERNS:**

Forex is a dynamic market where prices are always on a move, the price for any given pair moves towards or away from a specific area on the chart repeatedly. These movements lead to formation of some interesting price patterns which allow the traders to predict the next move with varying degree of certainty.

Some price patterns are continuation in nature while the others point towards a reversal move. The commonly seen patterns are;

1. Head and Shoulders
2. Reverse Head and Shoulders
3. Pennants
4. Ascending Triangle
5. Descending Triangle
6. Bull Flag
7. Bear Flag
8. Double Top or Bottom
9. Triple Top or Bottom

1. Head and Shoulders Pattern: It is also called a Head and Shoulders Top pattern. It is one of the most reliable technical patterns used by the traders. It consists of 3 peaks where the middle peak is called the head & the other two peaks are called the shoulders. This pattern is a bearish reversal pattern which often results in a bearish move upon the break of the neckline.

The USD/JPY weekly chart above illustrates a nice Head and Shoulder Top Pattern. The trade is entered upon the break of the neckline to the downside and the profit target is usually set equal to the height from the neckline to the top of the shoulder (usually the first shoulder, as both shoulders can be of different heights and angles as well). We enter at the close of the candle that breaks through the neckline and set our profit target equal to the height between the neckline and the shoulder, which in this case is 1000 pips. The profit target is successfully hit in the chart above.

2. <u>Reverse Head and Shoulders Pattern:</u>   It is also called a Head and Shoulders Bottom pattern. Like the Head and Shoulder Top this is also a reliable technical pattern used by the traders. It consists of 3 peaks where the middle peak is called the head & the other two peaks are called the shoulders. This pattern is a bullish reversal pattern which often results in an upward move upon the break of the neckline.

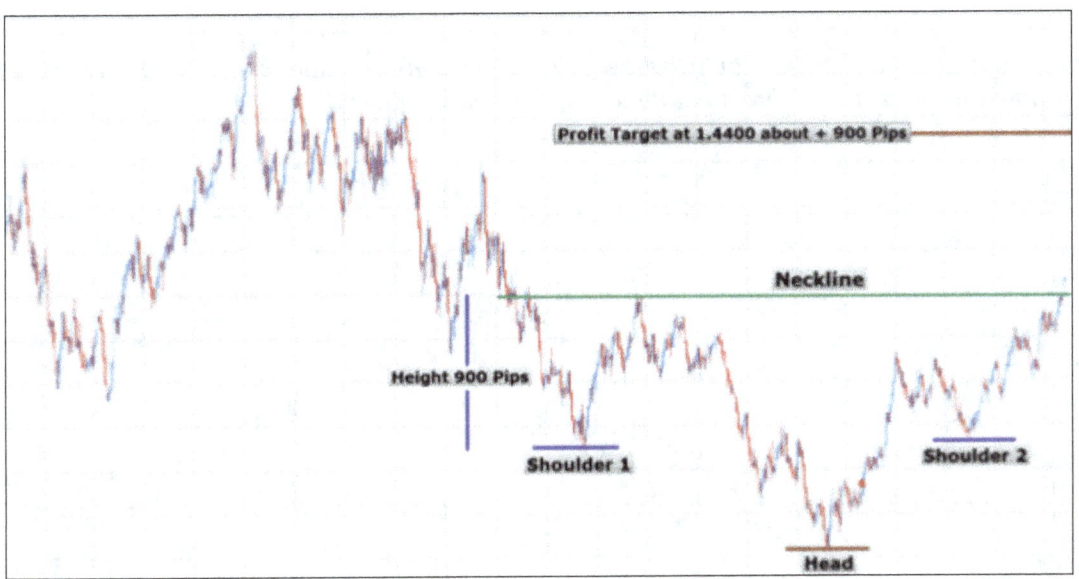

A reverse Head and Shoulder pattern has formed on the daily <u>EUR/USD</u> *chart above. The height between the shoulder and the neckline is about 900 pips therefore we will set our profit target at 1.4400 which is about 900 pips above the neckline. The pair has just broken above the neckline and I will be entering at the open of the next daily candle as we expect a bullish run on this pair. It is 10:00 PM in the evening, I will take a break here and will be back tomorrow, but before I start tomorrow I will update you on this trade.*

Good evening to all, as promised, let me update you on the trade listed above. The trade is working as expected; EUR/USD is on a tear the price has moved up to 1.3626 from an entry price of 1.3568 yesterday.

3. <u>Pennant:</u>   Pennants are continuation patterns; they can be bullish or bearish. Following a trend the price begins to consolidate between two oblique support and resistance levels thereby creating pennants. After a short period of consolidation the price breaks the pennant and usually continues in the direction of the original trend. The chart below is daily GBP/CHF chart. The initial bull run of the pair is interrupted by a pennant shown as price consolidation between the red and the green resistance and support lines respectively.

The chart below represents the initial bullish move followed by consolidation (pennant) and a break of price action from the pennant upwards in the direction of the original (bullish) trend.

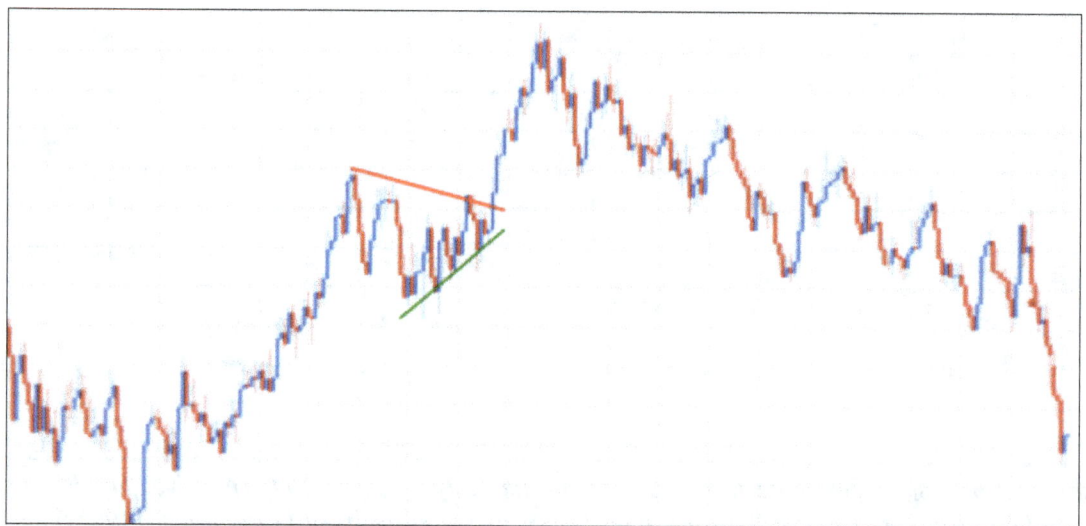

4. <u>Ascending Triangle:</u> An ascending triangle forms during an uptrend as it is a bullish continuation pattern. Following a bullish move the price starts to consolidate and if this consolidation happens between an oblique support and a horizontal resistance line then an ascending triangle is said to have formed. The price is projected to break the resistance line to the upside; therefore the long trade is entered upon the break of the resistance line. The protective stop is placed below the support line & the profit target is set at a level equal to the distance between the widest part of the triangle.

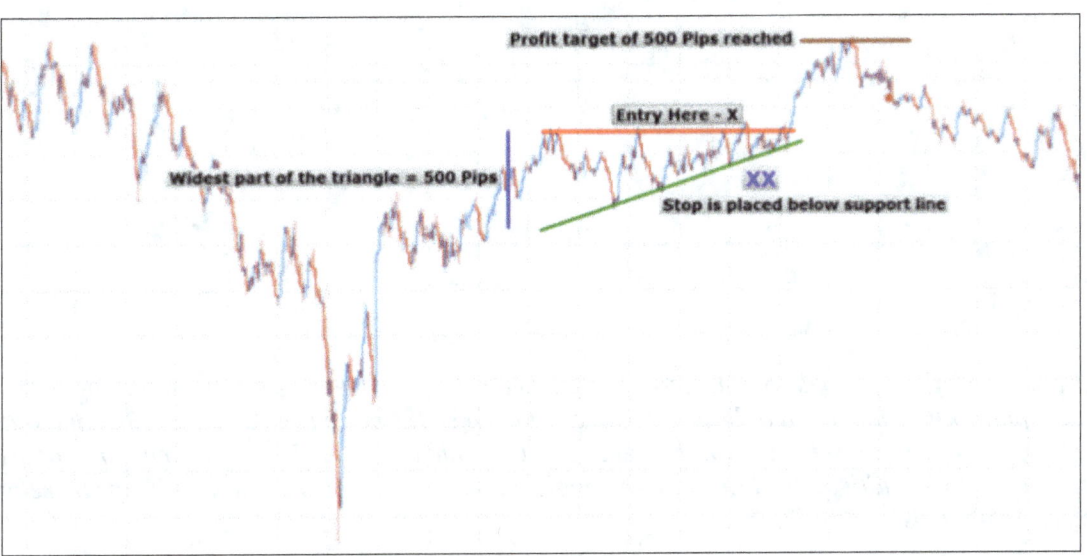

This chart above is a CAD/CHF daily chart, following a sharp bullish move the price starts oscillating between the green oblique support line and the red horizontal resistance line. Once the price breaks the resistance line we enter a long trade on CAD/CHF pair and set our profit target at 0.9900, which is about 500 pips from our resistance line. Please note that the maximum width of the ascending triangle on the CAD/CHF chart was 500 pips therefore we set our profit target at 500 pips.

5. <u>Descending Triangle:</u> A descending triangle forms during a downtrend as it is a bearish continuation pattern. Following a bearish move the price starts to consolidate and if this consolidation happens between an oblique resistance and a horizontal support line then a descending triangle is said to have formed. The price is projected to break the support line to the downside; therefore a short trade is entered upon the break of the support line. The protective stop is placed above the resistance line and the profit target is set at a level equal to the distance between the widest part of the triangle.

The chart above is a EUR/USD daily chart, following a bearish move the price starts oscillating between the green horizontal support line and the red oblique resistance line. Once the price breaks the support line we enter a short trade on EUR/USD pair and set our profit target at 1.2500, which is about 500 pips from our support line. Please note that the maximum width of the descending triangle on the EUR/USD chart was 500 pips therefore we set our profit target at 500 pips.

6. <u>Bull Flag:</u> A bull flag forms during an up-trend as it is a bullish continuation pattern. Following a bullish move the price starts to consolidate between parallel, oblique support and resistance lines. The pattern resembles a flag therefore the name bull flag. The price is projected to break the resistance line to the upside; therefore a long trade is entered upon the break of the resistance line. The protective stop is placed below the support line & the profit target is set at a level equal to the width of the channel.

The chart above is a USD/CHF daily chart, following a strong bullish move the price starts oscillating between an oblique channel bounded by a parallel green support line and a red resistance line. Once the price breaks the resistance line we enter a long trade on the USD/CHF pair and set our profit target 350 pips from entry, because the maximum width of the oblique channel is 350 pips.

7. <u>Bear Flag:</u>   A bear flag forms during a downtrend as it is a bearish continuation pattern. Following a bearish move the price starts to consolidate   between parallel, oblique support and resistance lines. The pattern resembles an inverted flag therefore the name bear flag. The price is projected to break the support line to the downside; therefore a short trade is entered upon the break of the support line. The protective stop is placed above the resistance line & the profit target is set at a level equal to the width of the channel.

Disclaimer: The content on this page is for educational purposes only and should not be construed in any way as trading advice. The risk of loss in online trading of stocks, Forex, options, and foreign equities is substantial.

The chart above is a <u>USD/CHF</u> weekly chart, following a strong bearish move the price starts oscillating between an oblique channel bounded by a parallel green support line and a red resistance line. Once the price breaks the support line we enter a short trade on the <u>USD/CHF</u> pair and set our profit target 900 pips from entry, because the maximum width of the oblique channel is 900 pips.

      8. <u>Double Top and Bottom:</u>   Double Tops and Bottoms are mirror images of one another and are bearish and bullish reversal patterns respectively. In the Double Top pattern the price hits the resistance line, fails to breaks through it and reverses back down to the support level. In the Double Bottom pattern the price hits the support level twice, fails to break through it, and reverses up to the resistance level.

There are two common ways of trading a double top or double bottom, some traders will enter the trade upon failure of the price action to pierce the resistance line or support lines respectively for the second time, they will stay short or long till the price reaches the support or support line & once the break occurs then the price level is expected to at least reach a distance equal to the width of the channel. The others wait and enter a short or long trade once the price action breaks the support or resistance line before entering the trade.

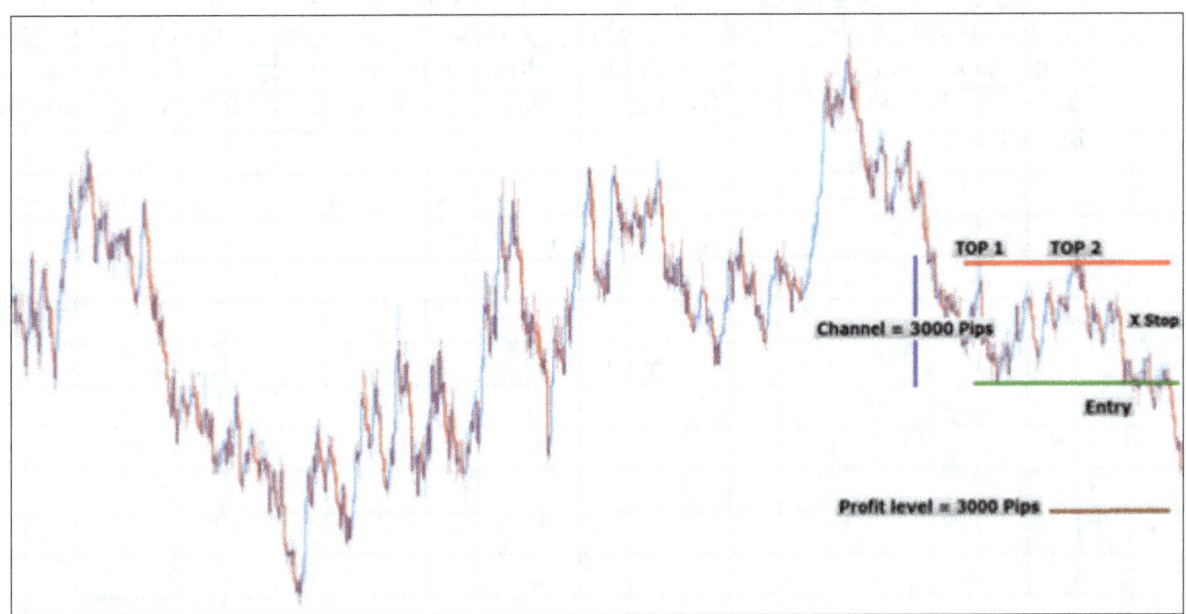

The chart above is a USD/SEK (US dollar/Swedish krona) daily chart, after forming a double top the price drops towards the support and then breaks through the support and moves towards the profit target which is equal to the width of the channel.

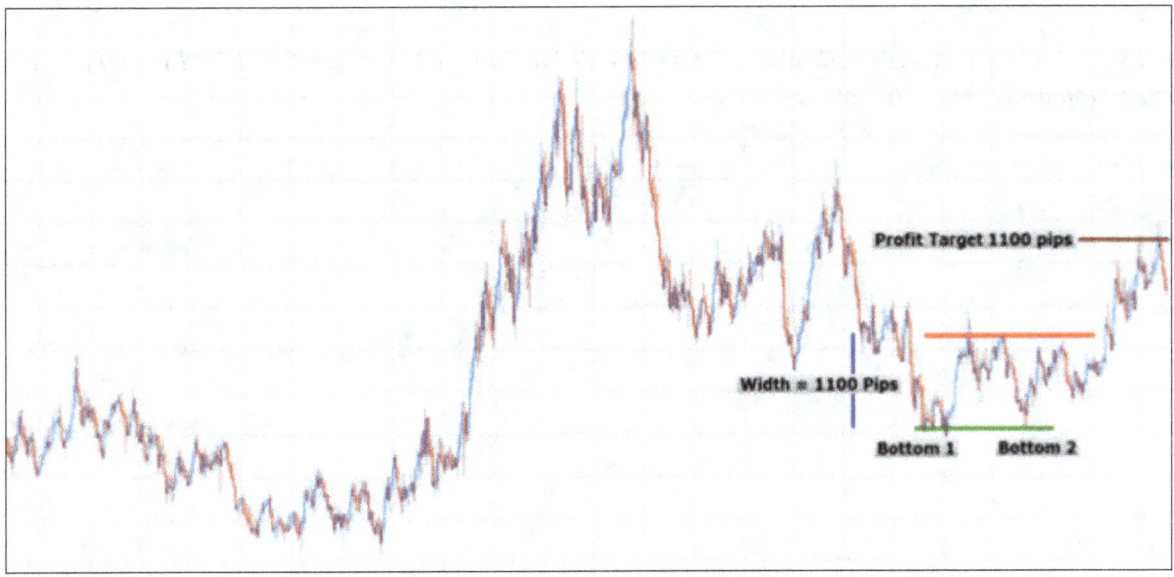

The daily chart above of EUR/HUF (Euro/Hungarian Forint) illustrates the Double Bottom pattern. The price breaks the resistance level and reached the profit target of 1100 pips

9. <u>Triple Top and Bottom:</u> Triple Tops and Bottoms are quite similar to a Double Top and Double Bottom pattern. As the name suggests the price hits the resistance and support level thrice respectively. The method of entry, setting up the profit target and placing a protective stop is similar to the Double Top and Double Bottom pattern. The following charts illustrate this pattern.

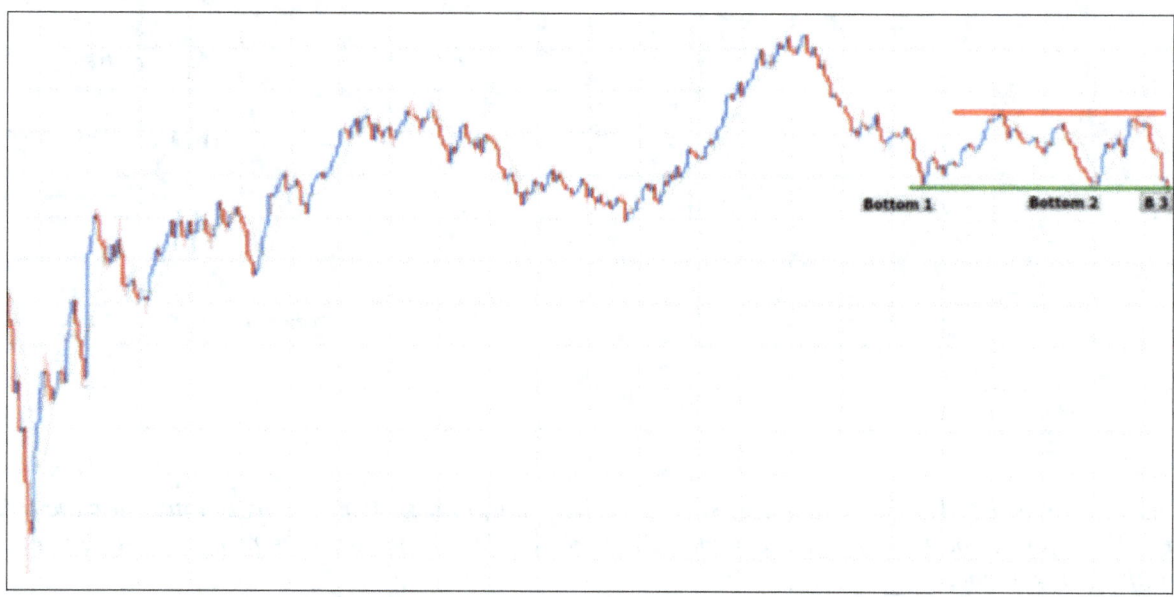

The daily AUD/CHF chart above illustrates formation of a Triple Bottom. On the chart I would like you to mark the entry, stop and take profit levels.

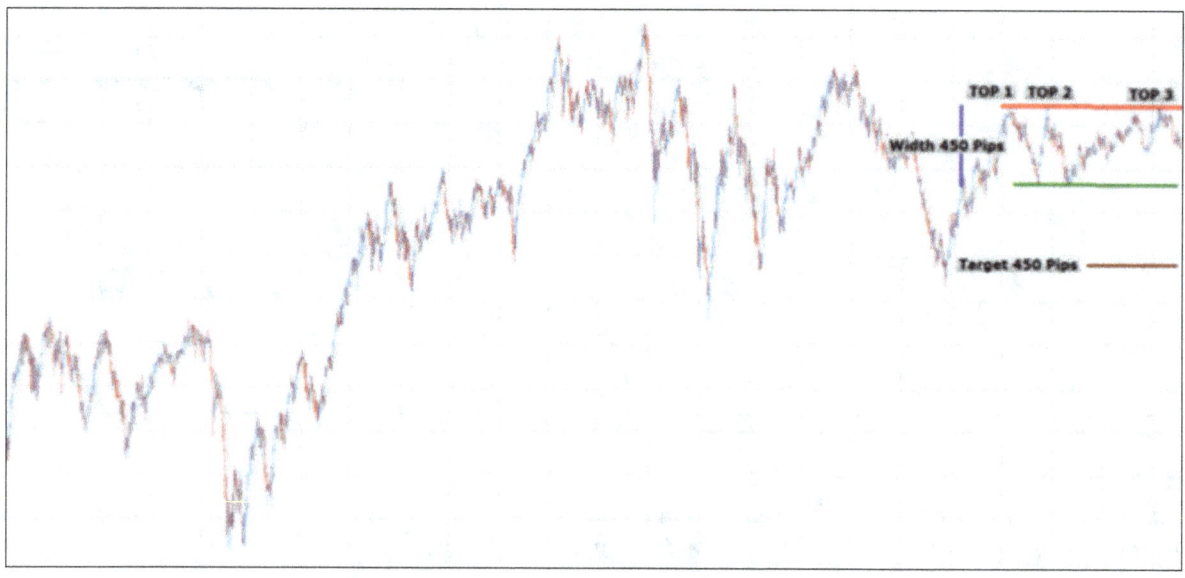

Disclaimer: The content on this page is for educational purposes only and should not be construed in any way as trading advice. The risk of loss in online trading of stocks, Forex, options, and foreign equities is substantial.

The AUD/USD chart on the previous page represents an example of a triple top.

WORD OF CAUTION: *It is very likely that the trades we enter based on the above mentioned technical patterns goes against our plan and end up as a losing trade. For every successful trade there is a possibility of quite a few losing trades. The examples shown above were specifically picked by me to illustrate the patterns. My purpose for writing this book was to educate individuals on the principles of Forex investing and develop a trading plan which will significantly reduce risk and puts us in a position to gain maximum profits irrespective of which way the market moves or how random the market is. The next two chapters are the ones which will introduce you to the practical applications of Forex investing.*

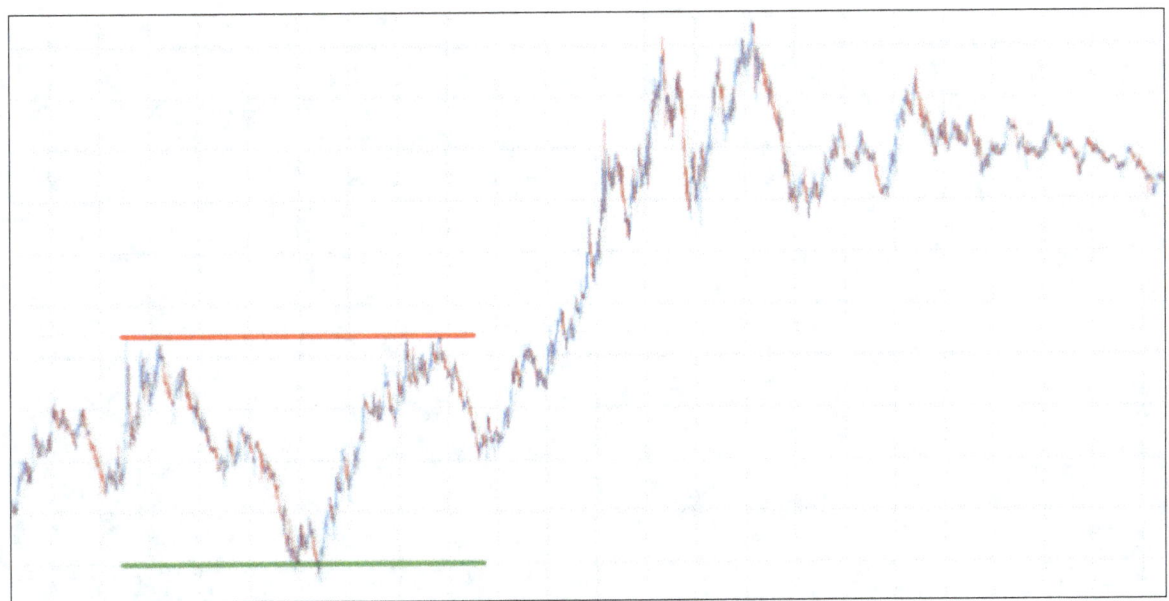

USD/TRY daily chart above shows a failed double top pattern trade. The price after hitting the resistance for the second time moves back towards the support but half way through the channel sharply changes direction and moves back up and breaks the resistance line.

PRACTICAL APPLICATIONS

CHAPTER SIX

PRACTICAL APPLICATIONS

Are you comfortable with the basic concepts of Forex investing as explained in the earlier chapters? Do you recognize the common currency pairs? Can you differentiate between a short and a long trade, bear and bull move? Does a candlestick Forex chart make sense to you? Would you be able to define the terms like pip, spread, lots, margin, leverage, and also determine the different units of a currency pair you can trade based upon the value of your account. If the answer to any of these questions is "NO" then I would strongly recommend that you revise the first five chapters of this book again. There is no harm in spending some more time on the theory as this will make your understanding more clear and will make the last two chapters more palatable and enjoyable to read and follow.

Are we ready? Did I hear yes! OK then let us proceed.

First we need a reliable computer, desktop or a laptop doesn't matter, with a high speed Internet network connections. The old dial-in Internet set up is not recommended. Desktop or a laptop with the following specifications will suffice, in-addition the software requirements are also listed below:

    Desktop: 500 GB Hard Drive (Giga Byte)
                   2 – 4 GB memory
                   Fast Processor preferably 1.3 – 2.4 GHz (Giga Hertz)
                   Ethernet for fast wired Internet connection
                   Wireless Network card for wireless Internet connection

    Laptop: 320 GB Hard Drive (Giga Byte)
                   2 GB or higher memory
                 Fast Processor preferably 1.3 – 2.4 GHz (Giga Hertz)
               Ethernet for fast wired Internet connection
               Wireless Network card for wireless Internet connection

    Software: Operating Systems: Mac OS X
                    Windows® 2000, XP, Vista or 7

                   Free Downloads: Java™ Sun Microsystems® Latest version
                   Adobe Flash Player® Version 10 or 11

Next I would like you to search for free Forex charts on the Internet and familiarize yourself with various pairs, their exchange rates, trends, ranges over the last few years. You should practice drawing trend lines, especially support and resistance lines, plotting some common indicators like Simple Moving Averages and Relative Strength Indicators (RSI) on these charts.

A few convenient and effective resources are found at: www.forexfactory.com/markets

Disclaimer: *The content on this page is for educational purposes only and should not be construed in any way as trading advice. The risk of loss in online trading of stocks, Forex, options, and foreign equities is substantial.*

Please note that I have no connection with these sites and do not guarantee the accuracy of content on these sites. The sites are mentioned here for reference and educational purpose only as they offer free content.

One of the disadvantages of working on these free sites is that you cannot save your chart set-ups, but for me that is fine because I would prefer that you open these charts at least once per day and practice drawing and plotting the trend lines and indicators respectively. You should be viewing the currency pairs on the hourly, daily and weekly time frames, reviewing these time frames will give you a detailed insight on the movements of these currency pairs. My expectations are that after a couple of weeks you will be able to determine that a given pair is either in an up-trend, downtrend or is consolidating. Always ask yourself this question when you review a daily Forex chart. You should also be able to draw a support or resistance lines without hesitation.

Please remember that you have to have at least two price point levels connected for your trend line to be valid. I also expect you to know the current exchange rates by heart of the Euro, Pound, Yen, Australian, New Zealand, Canadian dollars and Swiss Franc against the US dollar and the current exchange rate of Euro, Pound, US, Australian, New Zealand, Canadian dollars and Swiss Franc against the Yen, and also the exchange rate of Euro, Pound, Yen, US, Australian, New Zealand, and Canadian dollars against the Swiss Franc.

Please be assured that this is not a tough ask, as you review the Forex charts daily these exchange rates will get engrained in your memory in a couple of weeks, believe me even my grandma has memorized these rates. Also try to spot as many technical patterns and candlestick patterns as possible, these exercises will help train your eyes to spot the patterns listed in Chapter 5 and you can follow these patterns in real life to see how they play out.

I would also like you to follow the important fundamental news for an economy on a regular basis. The majority of financial news sites list the weekly schedule of releases, with listing of the previous month figures and expectations for the current month's release. If the economic data is positive and beats the expectations then that specific currency gets a boost, but if the data is negative and below expectations then you expect the respective currency to suffer. One of the free sites that lists a weekly calendar of economic data releases and releases the current figures live is Forex Factory (www.forexfactory.com). This site is basically a forum where Forex traders share their ideas, trading strategies and relevant Forex current events.

Again please note that I have no collaboration with this site and do not guarantee the accuracy of content on this site. The site is mentioned here for reference and educational purpose only as they offer free content. I would suggest that you only follow their economic calendar, there might be some quality trading strategies but majority of the articles and news is likely to confuse you and distract you from focusing on proper Forex investing.

The following data is of importance and points towards the health of an economy:

- Gross Domestic Product (GDP): Positive and improving GDP reflects a growing economy and is positive for the currency. The GDP is released quarterly but there is monthly estimate release that can impact the specific currency.

- Consumer Price Index (CPI): Positive and improving CPI reflects rising inflation which is likely to lead to increasing interest rates which strengths the currency. Figures are released monthly

- Retail Sales: Positive and improving Retail Sales reflects a vibrant economy and is positive for the currency. Figures are released monthly

- Trade Balance: Positive and improving Trade Balance is good for the economy and is positive for the currency. Figures are released monthly

- Industrial Production: Positive and improving Industrial production number above 50 reflects a growing economy and is positive for the currency, while a figure below 50 represent economic contraction and has a negative impact on the specific currency. Figures are released monthly

- Employment Report: This report includes the unemployment rate and the number of jobs created during the previous month. Increasing job growth numbers and a falling unemployment figures are positive for an economy and its currency. This report is released monthly and here in USA the release of this report creates extreme volatility in the currency market.

- Consumer/Business Confidence: An increasing number represents confidence in the economy by the consumers and the businesses therefore the businesses are likely to invest in the economy and the individual consumer is likely to spend more thereby further boosting economic growth and well-being. This data is also released on a monthly basis.

- Housing Data: Rising home prices and a fall in home inventory represents a vibrant housing market. This indicates that the people are feeling confident about the economy and are willing to invest money in the housing sector. This data is also released monthly and a positive numbers support the respective currency.

- Central Bank Meetings/Interest Rate Decisions: Majority of Central Banks are scheduled to meet 9-12 times per year. During these meetings the overall health of the economy is reviewed, monetary policies are drafted or analyzed, the current inflation rates are looked upon and interest rates decisions are made.

Following these meetings the interest rates are announced and also a statement is released which provides guidance about the economy, inflation targets and future interest rate expectations. One of the primary responsibilities of a central bank is to maintain the inflation levels within the set inflation target which is usually between 2-3% annually. If the inflation is increasing at a higher rate than the Central Bank steps in and increases the interest rate to bring the CPI and consumer spending down, on the other hand if the inflation rates are low then it is very unlikely that the Central Bank will increase interest rates. Central banks are likely to cut interest rates if there is risk of deflation or shrinking economy. An increasing interest rate increases the yield for that specific currency as investors are likely to invest in the economy which offers a better rate of return.

I have an assignment for you here. Below I will list the names of all the major Central Bank current governors and would like you to memorize these names as their statements during policy meetings or press conferences carry a lot of weight and can move the Forex market significantly.

Serial Number	Central Bank	Chairman/Governor	Interest Rate
1	Federal Open Market Committee (FOMC) - USA	Ben Bernanke	< 0.25%
2	European Central Bank (ECB) President	Mario Draghi	0.75%
3	Bank of England (BOE)	Mark Carney	0.50%
4	Swiss National Bank (SNB)	Thomas Jordan	< 0.25%
5	Bank of Japan (BOJ)	Haruhiko Kuroda	<0.10%
6	Bank of Canada (BOC)	Stephen S. Poloz	1.00%
7	Reserve Bank of Australia (RBA)	Glenn Stevens	3.00%
8	Reserve Bank of New Zealand (RBNZ)	Graeme Wheeler	2.50%

Another name you need to be aware of is of the Japan's Finance Minister, Mr. Taro Aso. Japanese government is always keen on depreciating the Yen against other currencies therefore the Finance Minister frequently serves verbal volleys to that effect which the currency market usually pays attention to.

A sample schedule of next week's economic releases for the major economies is listed below:

[Economic calendar table showing events including Average Earnings Index 3m/y (GBP, 1.4%, 1.3%), Unemployment Rate (GBP, 7.8%, 7.8%), ZEW Economic Expectations (CHF, 2.2), German 10-y Bond Auction (EUR), Foreign Securities Purchases (CAD, 10.23B, 14.91B), Building Permits (USD, 1.00M, 0.99M), Housing Starts (USD, 0.93M, 0.91M), BOC Rate Statement (CAD), Overnight Rate (CAD, 1.00%, 1.00%), Fed Chairman Bernanke Testifies (USD), BOC Monetary Policy Report (CAD), Crude Oil Inventories (USD, -0.9M), BOC Press Conference (CAD), FOMC Member Raskin Speaks (USD), Beige Book (USD), CB Leading Index m/m (AUD, 0.3%), NAB Quarterly Business Confidence (AUD, 2), Trade Balance (CHF, 2.41B, 2.22B)]

Our next step is to open a trading account, before we do that we need to review the Forex brokers available and then determine who will best serve our needs of Forex investing. Our aim is to work with a broker who is transparent, provides good customer service, is well regulated, well-funded (at least have assets above the minimum threshold required by the regulators) and protects the interest of their clients rather than just focusing on their personal business interests. There are quite a few brokers to choose from, but the characteristics and features i look for in a broker or the trading platform offered are as follows:

_____ Regulated by CFTC (Commodity and Futures Trading Commission) & NFA (National Futures Association). In the UK by FSA (Financial   Services Authority)

_____ The broker is well funded. In the USA NFA requires Forex   dealers to have net capital reserves in excess of $ 20 million. The brokers who are unable to maintain these reserves are forced to close and relocate outside the USA

_____ Worldwide access to these regulated Forex dealers

_____ Easy to use Trading Platforms

_____ Availability of desktop, web based and mobile platforms

_____ Allows the ability to trade different lot sizes on a single platform.

_____ Allows demo and real time accounts

_____ Customer service available during trading hours

Disclaimer: *The content on this page is for educational purposes only and should not be construed in any way as trading advice. The risk of loss in online trading of stocks, Forex, options, and foreign equities is substantial.*

_____ Does not charge commission

_____ Swift execution of trades, ability to open and close trades promptly

_____ Allows adequate leverage. The maximum leverage allowed in USA is 50:1 while outside the USA the leverage can be as high as 200:1. *Please note there is a high risk of loss associated with higher leverage*

_____ Availability of Forex charts and economic news calendar along with the trading platforms

_____ Avoid *"Dealing Desk Forex brokers"* as they act as a counter party to your trades. The term dealing desk means that there is someone on the other end of the trade who takes counter positions against your trades. When your trade is successful, the dealer loses, and vice versa. There are speculations that dealing desk brokers tend to manipulate the prices, however this is difficult to confirm.

_____ I prefer *"Non Dealing Desk Forex brokers"* also referred to as Electronic Communication Network (ECN) and "Straight Through Processing" (STP) brokers. In other words, there are no dealing desks which means that when you place a trade, it is processed straight through to the interbank markets and your trades are processed that very instant.

I would like you to research your Forex broker before signing up, as most of the information is readily available on the net. I have a couple of preferred Forex brokers but my mention of them should not be construed in any way as recommendations.

Name	Headquarter/Year Founded	Website	Regulated	Minimum Deposit	Minimum Units of Trading	Demo and Live Accounts	Deposit With:
Oanda Corporation	New York, USA/ 1995	www.oanda.com	Yes	None	1 unit (1)	Yes	Bank wire, Check, Credit Card
FXCM Inc.	New York, USA/ 1999	www.fxcm.com	Yes	$50, for micro account, other accounts different	1 micro-lot (1000 units), Different account required to trade mini & full lot	Yes	Bank wire, Check, Credit Card
Forex.com	New York, USA/ 1999	www.Forex.com	Yes	$ 250 for mini accounts	1 micro-lot (1000 units)	Yes	Bank wire, Check, Credit Card
Citi Fx Pro	New York, USA/ 2008	citifxpro.com	Yes	$10,000.00	1 micro-lot (1000 units)	Yes	Bank wire, Check, Credit Card

We are now ready to open a practice account. As you can visualize from the chart above that the majority of Forex brokers offer practice accounts in addition to the real accounts to their clients. These demo accounts are free and are easy to open. The practice trading platforms are similar to the real account platforms in style, execution of trades, currency pairs, Forex charts and price movements. The only difference being that the demo platform comes laden with virtual money while the real account requires you to deposit funds in order for you to trade. These practice accounts are quite valuable for the traders who are new to Forex as they allow them to get accustomed to the layout of the platform, practice execution of trades, interpret Forex charts, manage trades and practice new trading strategies. It is important to note that the time spent on these demo trading platforms does not guarantee automatic success on the real accounts but will surely make you a smart trader.

Here I will demonstrate opening up a practice account.

Demo Account Broker # 1:

©2013 OANDA Corporation. Used with permission.

Go to OANDA® home page at www.OANDA.com
Click on "Forex Trading"

Then Click "Sign in to fxTrade Practice"
Click "Sign Up"

From the drop down list select "Free Demo Account" under "Product" section, complete all required information.

Disclaimer: *The content on this page is for educational purposes only and should not be construed in any way as trading advice. The risk of loss in online trading of stocks, Forex, options, and foreign equities is substantial.*

As discussed earlier at the beginning of this unit, I am now going to demonstrate opening a demo account with a broker. (©2013 OANDA Corporation. The following images Used with permission.)

Go to <u>OANDA</u>® home page at www.OANDA.com
Click on "Forex Trading"

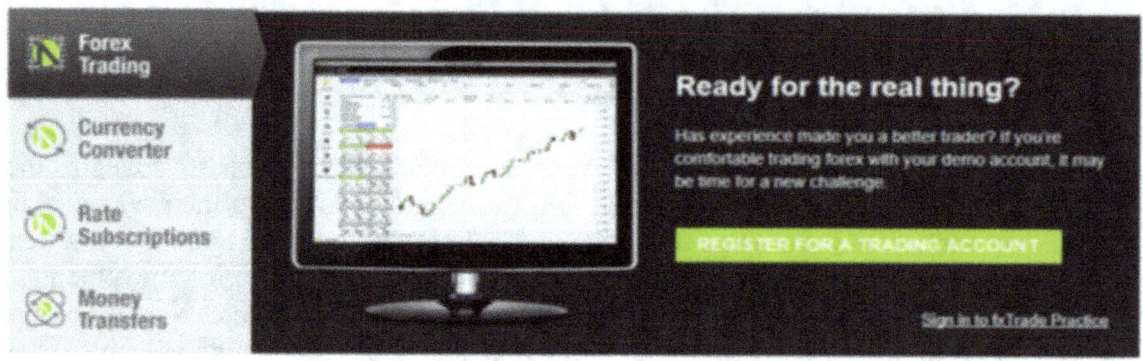

Then Click "Sign in to fxTrade Practice"

84

Disclaimer: The content on this page is for educational purposes only and should not be construed in any way as trading advice. The risk of loss in online trading of stocks, Forex, options, and foreign equities is substantial.

Then Click "Sign in to fxTrade Practice"
Click "Sign Up"

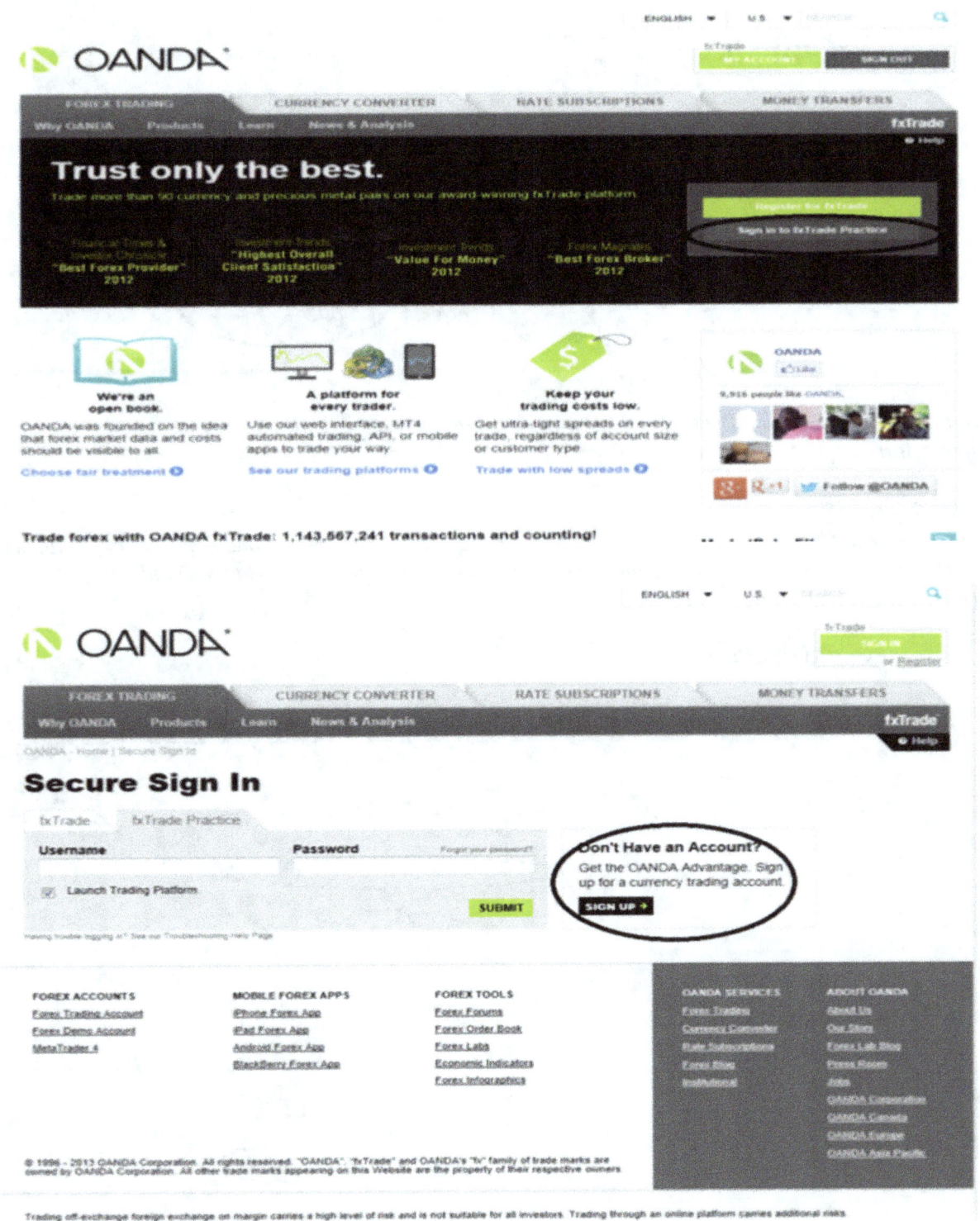

Click "Sign Up"

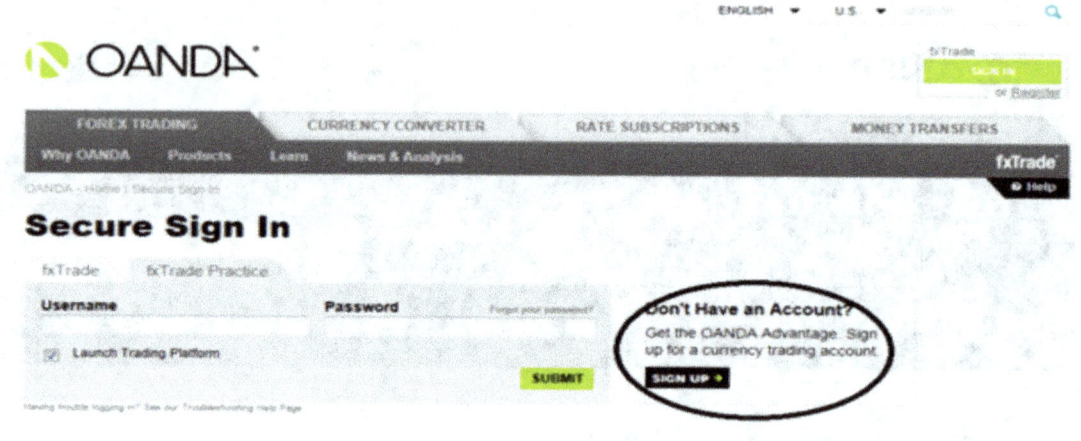

From the drop down list select "Free Demo Account" under "Product" section, complete all required information.

Click "Register"
*Remember your "user-name" and "password" you entered. You immediately receive an email with further instructions. Activate your demo account by clicking on the link sent to you via the email.

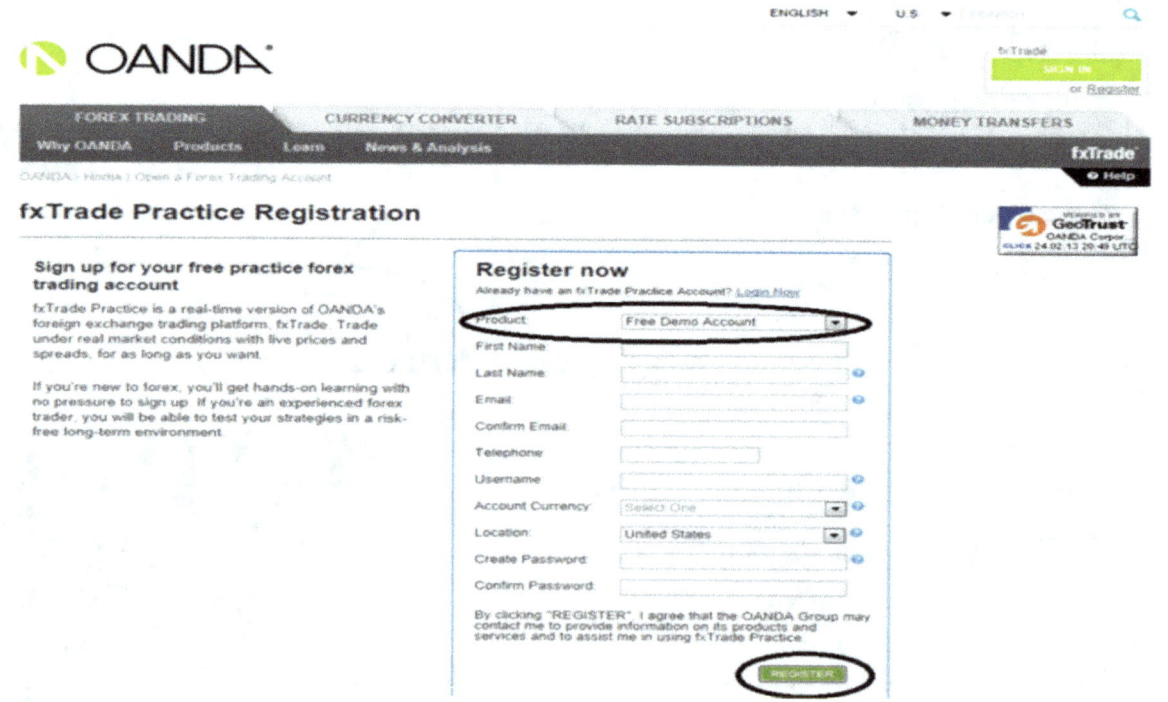

Characteristics of OANDA® Platform:

- Ability to trade even a single unit. Suitable for individuals who want to start with a small capital e.g. $ 100
- Can trade from 1 unit to even up to 100,000 units if you have enough funds in your account
- Forex charts embedded in the same window as the currency pairs and open trades.
- Easy to draw trend lines and apply indicators. You can always save your chart set ups
- Ability to open sub accounts within the same platform. Under current trading rules in USA, <u>hedging</u> is not allowed, i.e. you cannot open e.g. a Long EUR/USD position at the same time as a short EUR/USD position on a single platform, but with the ability to create sub accounts you can have a Long EUR/USD position open in one account and a short EUR/USD position open in the other sub account within the same platform.
- Another prevalent rule in US is the FIFO (first in first out) rule, which means that if you have multiple positions open for a single currency pair then you are required to first close the trades which was entered first or close all the trades for that pair at the same time
- You are paid interest on your deposit on a daily basis in addition to the swap on open trades.
- OANDA® demo account comes with an initial balance of $ 100,000 of demo money
- You can either download a "desk-top" icon or long in to the demo account via the Oanda® website.

- The trading platform will open with the default lay out. Next we will customize the platform for the sake of simplicity and analyze various areas on the platform. **<u>Java® download is required in order for the platform to open</u>**
- Finally we will execute some random practice trades and review our results

---

Disclaimer: *The content on this page is for educational purposes only and should not be construed in any way as trading advice. The risk of loss in online trading of stocks, Forex, options, and foreign equities is substantial.*

Setting Up OANDA® Trading Platform:

Visit the OANDA® homepage, www.OANDA.com
Click "sign in to fxtrade practice"

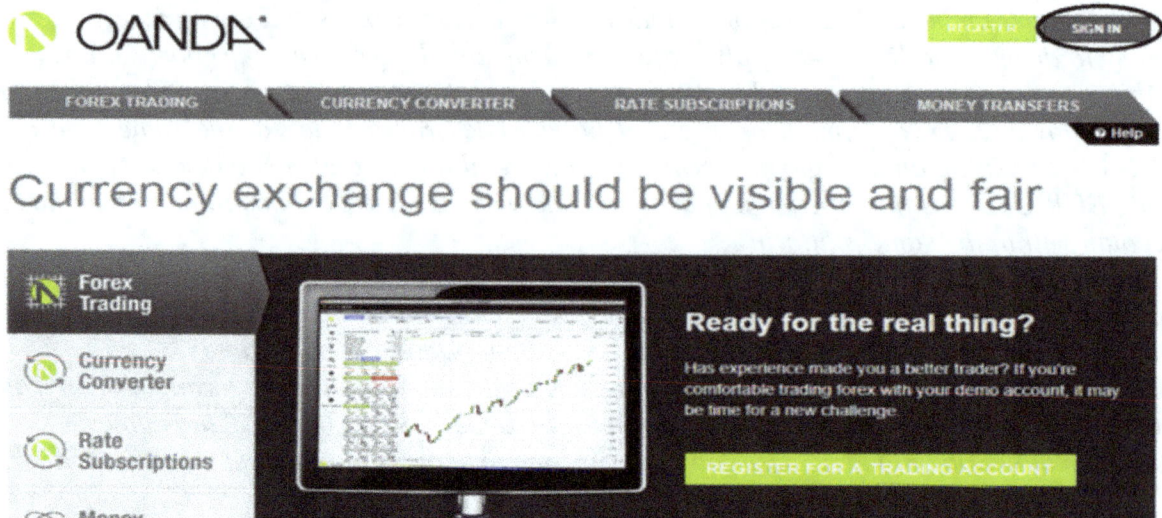

Enter your user-name and password; also make sure to check the box next to "Launch Trading Platform"

Click "Submit"

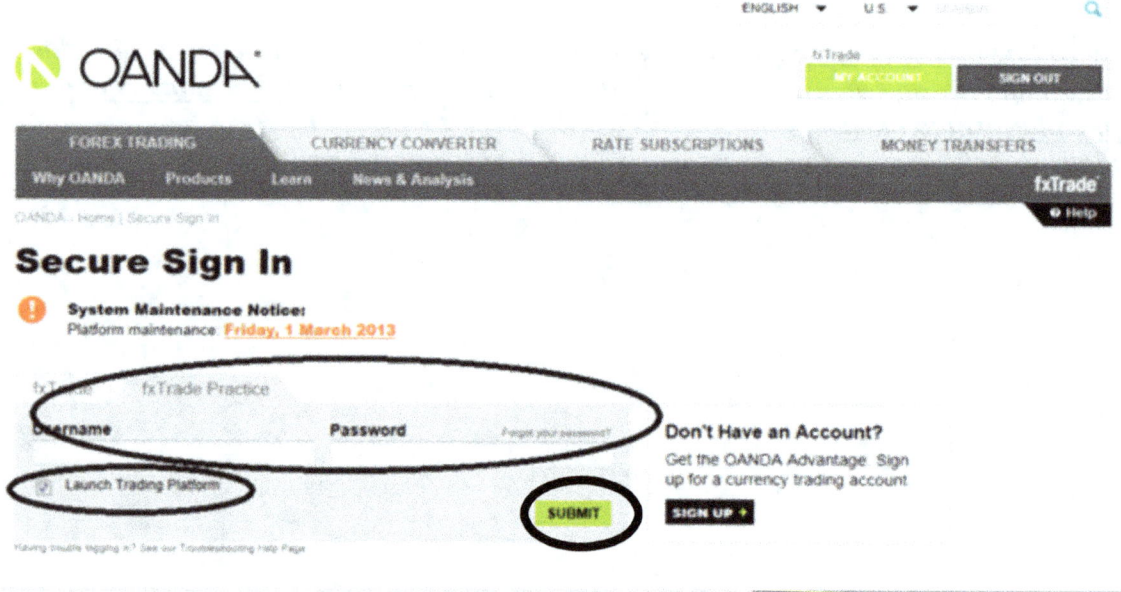

88

Disclaimer*: The content on this page is for educational purposes only and should not be construed in any way as trading advice. The risk of loss in online trading of stocks, Forex, options, and foreign equities is substantial.*

Next Click *"LAUNCH FXTRADE PRACTICE"*.

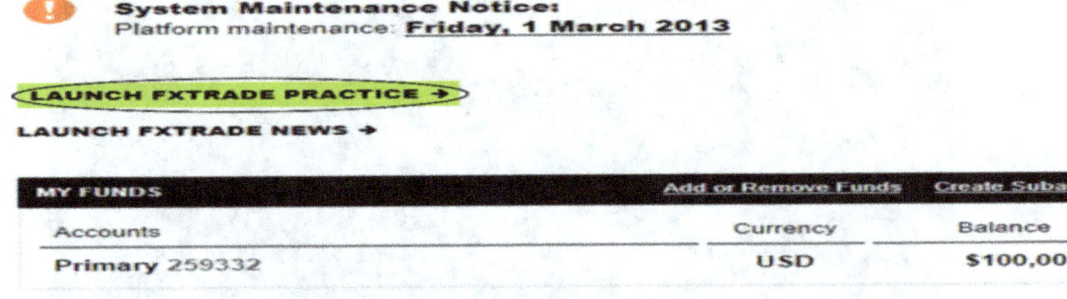

The new window will start loading the platform if your computer has java® installed on your computer. If the platform does not open then you will need to install java plug in.

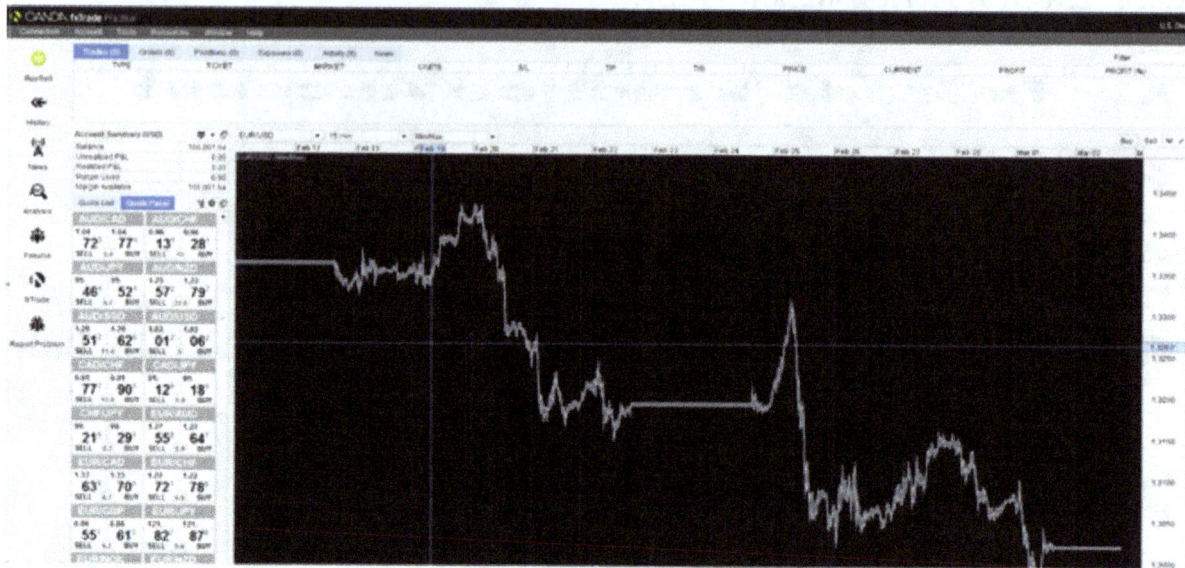

The demo platform opens up in a default form. Let us customize the platform for simplicity purposes. There are **5** key areas of the platform

1. <u>*Tool bar for functionality Section:*</u>

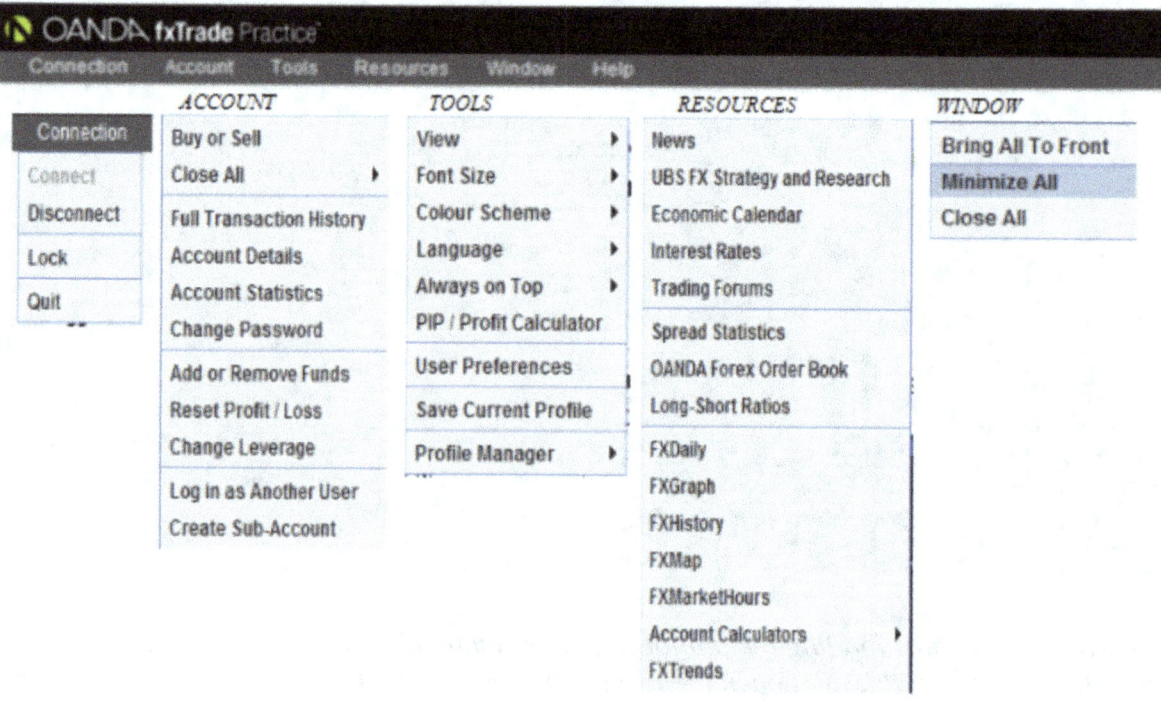

2. *Account Summary Section:*

Account Summary (USD)	
Balance	100,001.64
Unrealized P&L	0.00
Realized P&L	0.00
Margin Used	0.00
Margin Available	100,001.64

The information showing in the above window is enough, but in order to view more information, expands this section by clicking the area, as circled above.

Account Summary (USD)	
Balance	100,001.64
Unrealized P&L	0.00
Unrealized P&L (%)	0.00
Net Asset Value	100,001.64
Margin Alert	n/a
Realized P&L	0.00
Margin Used	0.00
Margin Available	100,001.64
Margin Closeout Value	100,001.65
Margin Closeout Percent (%)	n/a
Position Value	0.00

We are going to discuss this section in detail once we have a demo trade open. Did you notice that our "Balance" in the Account Summary section shows $ 100,001.64, when actually this demo account came with a demo amount of $ 100,000 and we have not taken any trades, so why do we see an increase in our balance? Anybody's guess? As I mentioned early the OANDA® platform offers interest on your deposit on a daily balance and as I opened this demo account about a week ago therefore that daily interest of $ 0.2740 on $ 100,000 has added up to $ 1.64 as of today.

3. *Currency Pairs Section:*

>We can view this section as "Quote Panel" or as a "Quote List". I usually prefer to view the pair in the Quote List Format

Quote Panel View

This view shows the Sell price e.g. AUD/CAD at 1.0472, Buy price e.g. AUD/CAD at 1.0477 and the Spread for this pair which at the moment is 5.4 pips

Quote List View

To view this format, Click on "Quote List"

This view allows us to view most of the selected currency pairs, it displays the Sell price, Buy price and the Spread for the currency pair in a different format.

Quote List	Quote Panel		
AUD/CAD	1.0472^5 / 77^9	5.4	▲
AUD/CHF	0.9613^1 / 28^1	15	
AUD/JPY	95.46^4 / 52^1	5.7	
AUD/NZD	1.2357^2 / 79^7	22.5	
AUD/SGD	1.2651^2 / 62^8	11.4	
AUD/USD	1.0201^2 / 06^2	5	
CAD/CHF	0.9177^2 / 90^1	12.9	
CAD/JPY	91.12^9 / 18^5	5.6	
CHF/JPY	99.21^6 / 29^9	8.3	
EUR/AUD	1.2755^8 / 64^7	8.9	
EUR/CAD	1.3363^9 / 70^6	6.7	
EUR/CHF	1.2272^1 / 78^6	6.5	
EUR/GBP	0.8655^2 / 61^5	6.3	
EUR/JPY	121.82^2 / 87^8	5.6	
EUR/NOK	7.4903^3 / 53^3	50	
EUR/NZD	1.5769^5 / 99^5	30	
EUR/PLN	4.1353^1 / 403^1	50	
EUR/SEK	8.3804^1 / 54^1	50	
EUR/TRY	2.3391^3 / 421^3	30	
EUR/USD	1.3018^4 / 21^7	3.3	
GBP/AUD	1.4732^3 / 44^5	12.2	
GBP/CAD	1.5435^1 / 44^0	8.9	
GBP/CHF	1.4171^8 / 86^8	15	
GBP/JPY	140.69^9 / 77^9	8	
GBP/NZD	1.8211^2 / 50^5	39.3	
GBP/USD	1.5036^1 / 41^1	5	
NZD/CAD	0.8460^1 / 75^1	15	
NZD/CHF	0.7766^4 / 88^8	22.4	

OANDA® offers a lot more pairs than FXCM ®. In order to display more pairs on your platform, Click on the "mechanical wheel" at the top of this section, as circled in red above.

Disclaimer: The content on this page is for educational purposes only and should not be construed in any way as trading advice. The risk of loss in online trading of stocks, Forex, options, and foreign equities is substantial.

Select the pairs you want to add under "ALL" list

Click "Add"

Selected pairs will move to the "Quote List"

Click "Save" and then Click "Apply"

Your selected pairs will be added to the platform

To remove a pair repeat the same steps in reverse

Please note that the OANDA® platform also allows you to trade Precious metals like Gold (XAU) and Silver (XAG). Gold and Silver is traded on a 1:1 leverage, while for the majority of other pairs a default leverage of 50:1 is set. You can reduce the leverage to a lower level by Clicking on "Change Leverage" under "Account" tab on the Toolbar.

In order to trade one unit of Gold you have to set aside approximately $1575 as a margin, as the current price of Gold is around $ 1575/ounce. If the price moves up to $ 1620/ounce then you are required to set aside a margin of $ 1620 in order to trade one unit of Gold. In order to trade one unit of Silver a margin of approximately $ 29 is required, as the current price of Silver is $ 29/ounce.

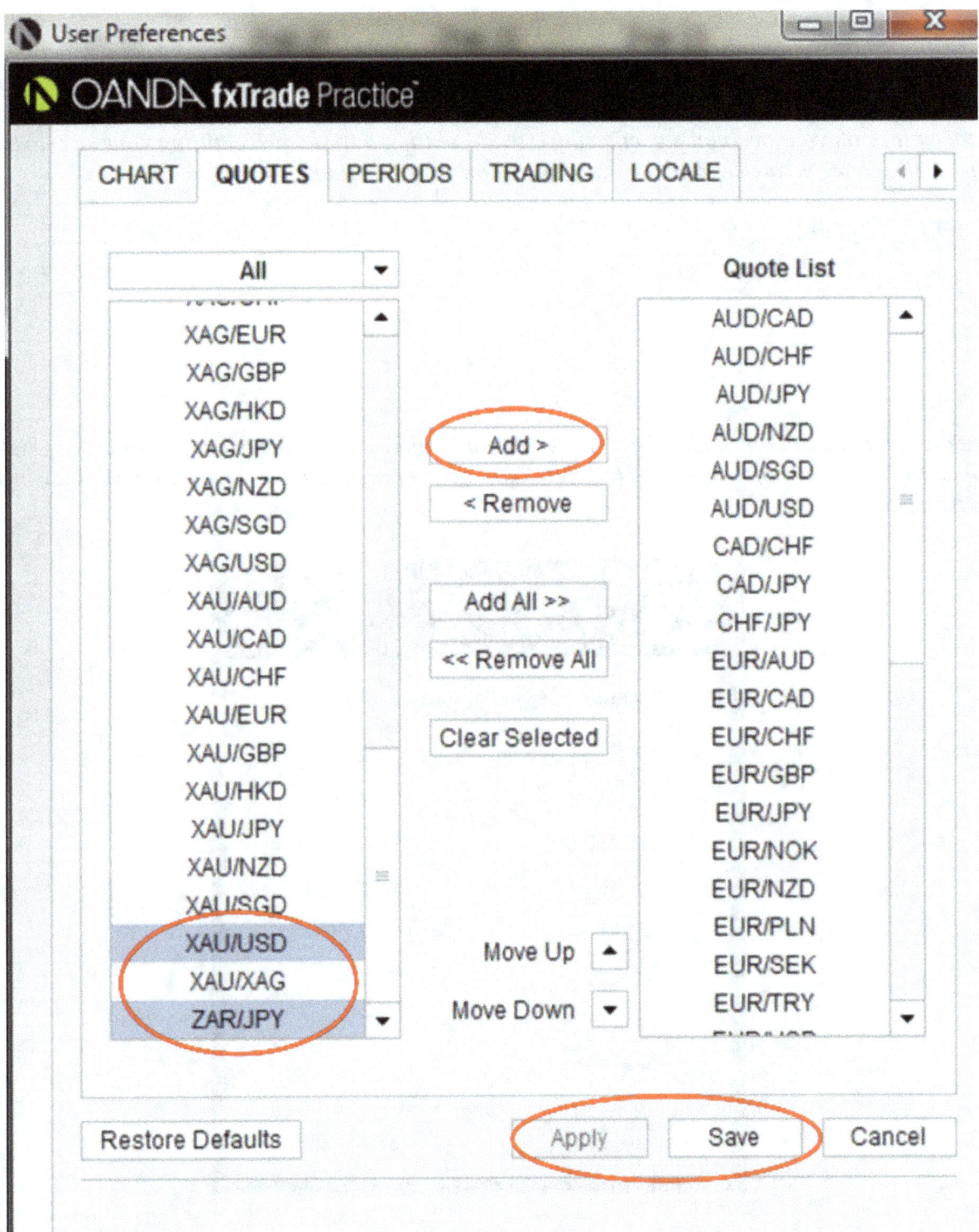

4. *Trade Section:*

This section shows your current open trades (Trades Tab), and your pending orders under "Orders" Tab. You are also able to review your cumulative open positions on each currency pair under "Position" Tab and exposure to each currency under "Exposure" Tab. The "Activity" Tab lists all the activities that take place on your account e.g. entering a trade, exiting a trade, price hitting your stop loss or take profit levels, canceled orders and the daily swaps on your positions.

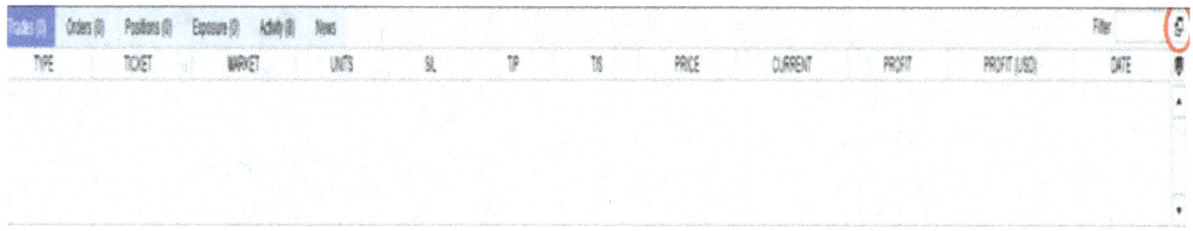

There are a lot of sub Tabs under the "Trade Section" and we need to customize this area. Click on the graph at top right area of this section (circled Red). Select only the sub tabs which have relevance to the open trades.

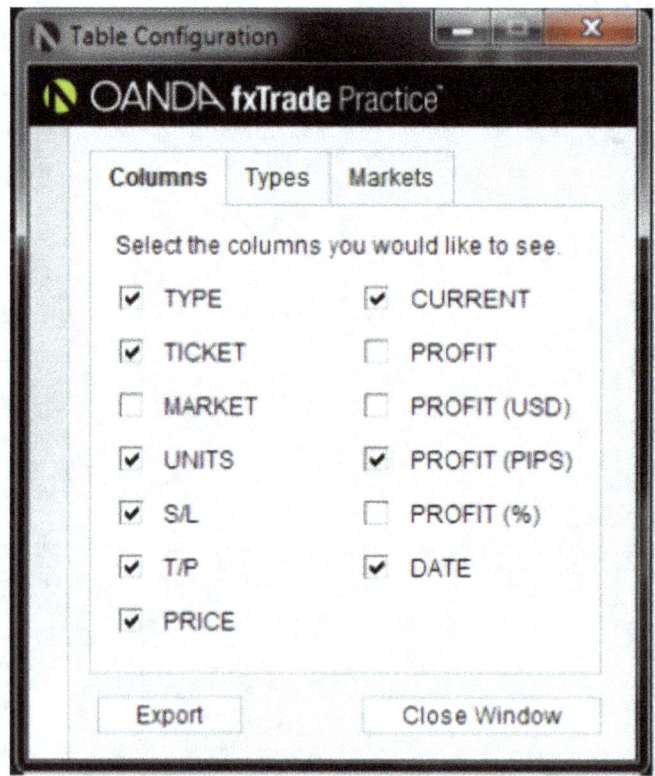

96

Disclaimer*: The content on this page is for educational purposes only and should not be construed in any way as trading advice. The risk of loss in online trading of stocks, Forex, options, and foreign equities is substantial.*

I will recommend to check the TYPE (long or short), TICKET #, UNITS (of a pair traded), S/L (stop loss level), T/P (take profit level) PRICE (the price level at which the trade was entered, CURRENT (current price of the pair entered), PROFIT (PIPS) (current profit in pips) and DATE (date position entered). Then click "Close Window" and your choices of sub Tabs will be displayed.

5. *Forex Chart Section:*

This area allows you to open the chart of the currency pairs that are active in your "Quote List". You can also select the "Time-frame" and the "Type" of chart you want displayed for a currency pair. My recommendations are to review the candlestick charts in a hourly or a daily time-frame.

After customizing the chart, adjust the width of the candles by Clicking on the "+" once at the bottom right of the chart (circled Red on the full chart shown on the following page)

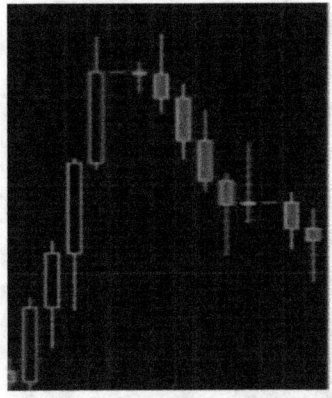

The Black candles with white border are bullish candles indicating the upward move in the price of a pair while the Gray candles are bearish candles that represent the downward move in the price of a pair.

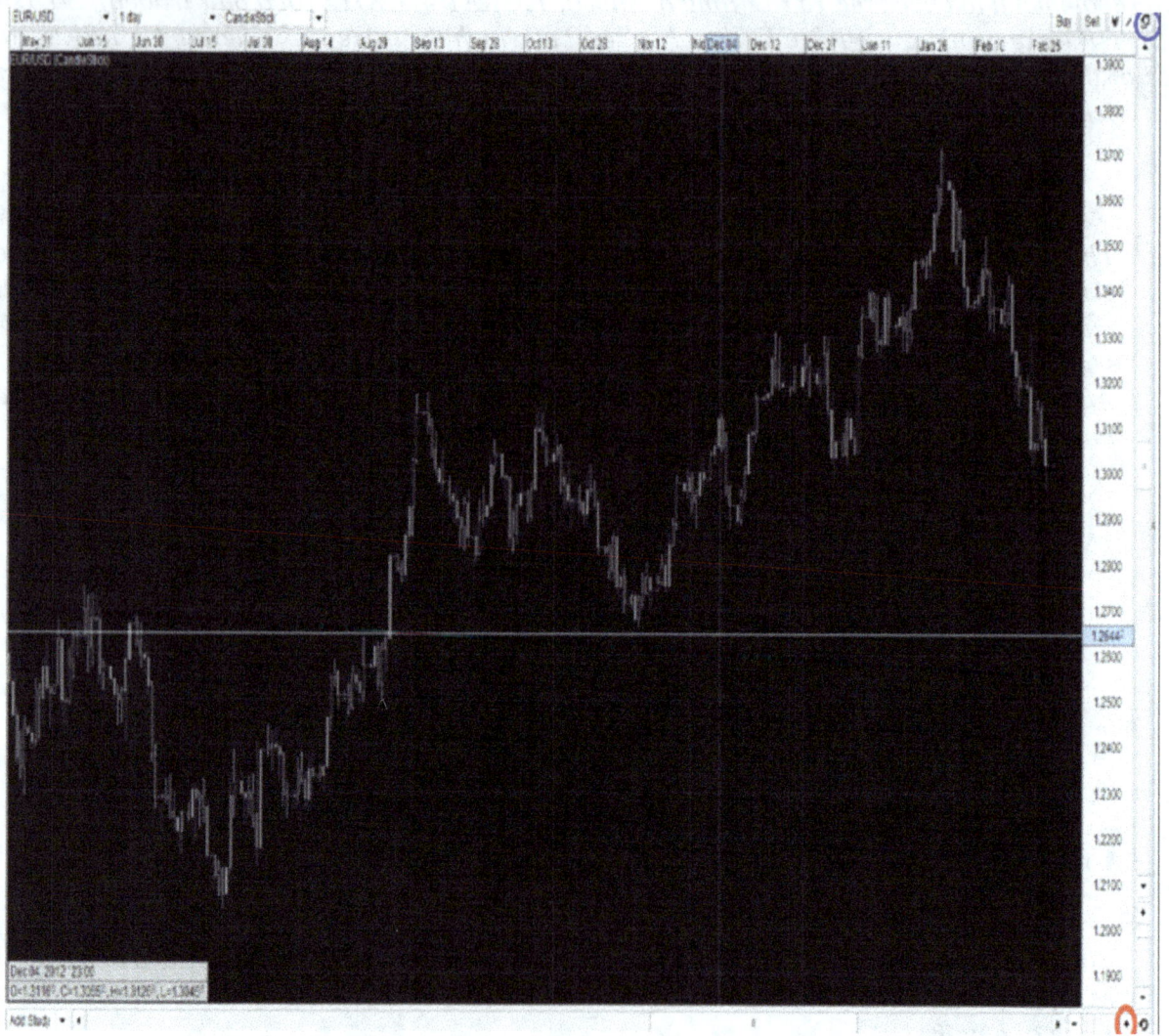

    At the bottom left of the chart the "Add Study" area allows you to add common Indicators to your charts. These indicators have default settings which can be changed as per your needs.

    An area at the top right of the chart (circled Blue in the chart above) allows you to draw trend lines and Fibonacci retracements.

Upon customization of the platform, setting up charts, adding trend lines and indicators, Save this Profile, so that the desired settings are not lost during the sign out process.

To change the color and the style of a trend line or an indicator, just right click on the respective trend line or an indicator and then choose the desired color and style.

SAVING PROFILE:

Click on "Tools"

Click "Profile Manager"

Click "Save Current Profile As"

Name your Profile and Click "Save"

In order to save future changes, go to "Tools" and Click on Save Current Profile" every time you make a change.

The default settings are always saved as "Primary"

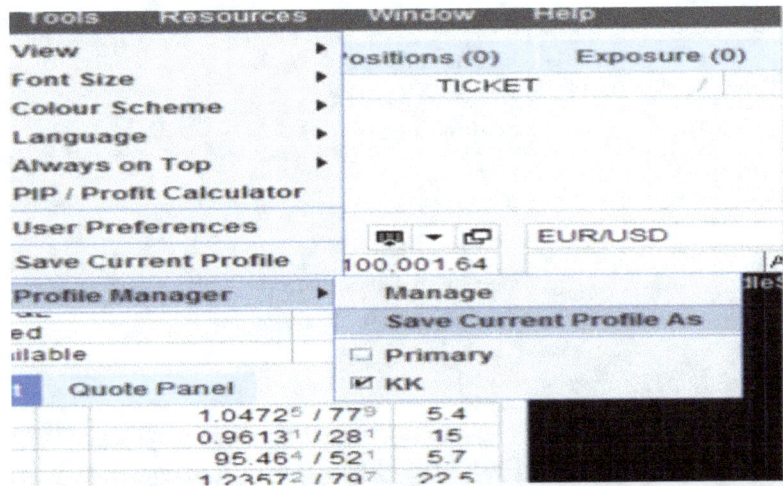

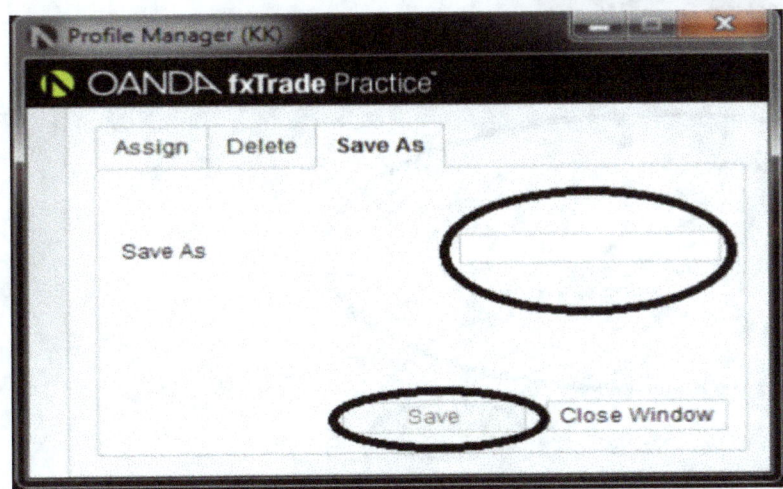

Before I demonstrate a sample trade on the OANDA® Platform let us create a sub-account, in case we need it later on for trading purposes.

CREATE SUB ACCOUNT:

Click on "Account"

Click "Create Sub Account"

A new window opens, complete the required information and Click "Submit".

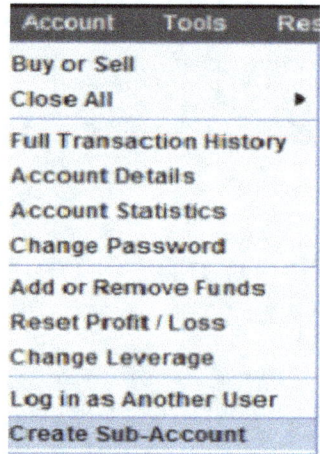

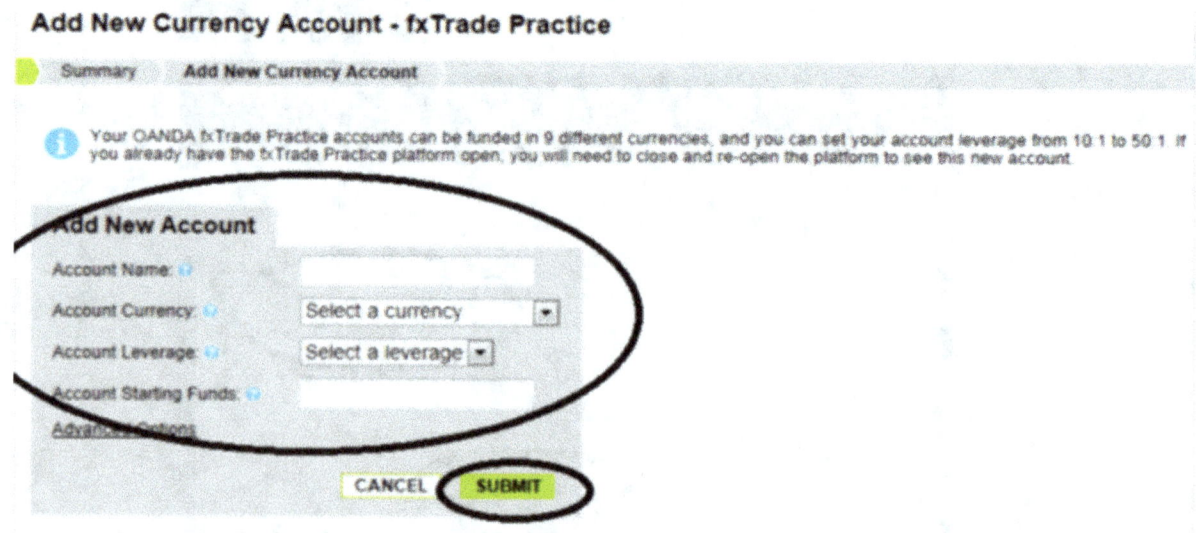

100

Disclaimer: The content on this page is for educational purposes only and should not be construed in any way as trading advice. The risk of loss in online trading of stocks, Forex, options, and foreign equities is substantial.

Your sub-account is now set up now. You will have to log out and log back in order to see the sub-account.

> Once you log back in, Click "Tools"
>
> Click "Profile Manager"
>
> Click on the "Name" you saved your Profile under, in order to view your customized platform
>
> Click on "Account"
>
> Click on "Change Account"

Now you are able to see the sub-account you created. **_Un-check "Change Profiles on Switch"_**

> Click on the account you want to open.

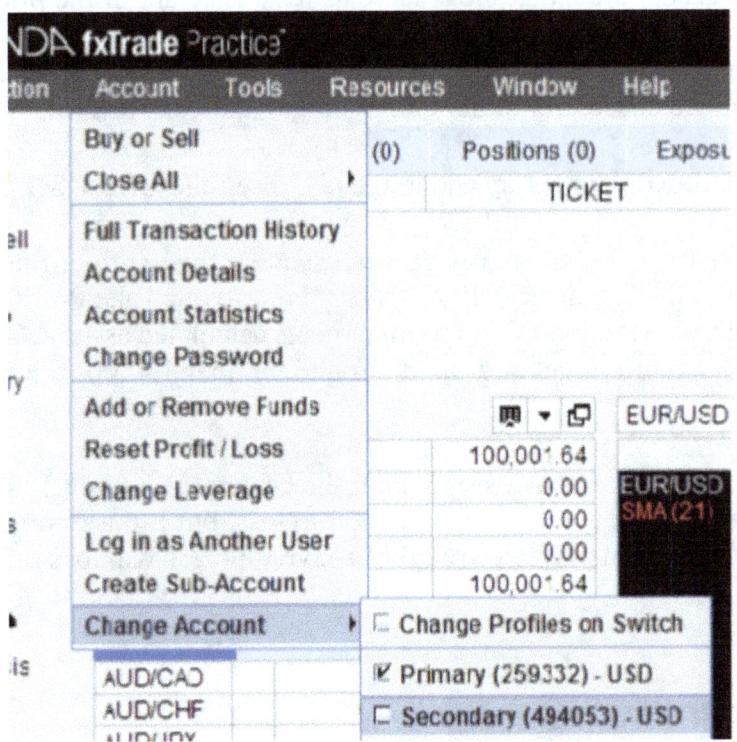

Remember you can create many sub-accounts on a single "OANDA®" Platform.

Disclaimer: The content on this page is for educational purposes only and should not be construed in any way as trading advice. The risk of loss in online trading of stocks, Forex, options, and foreign equities is substantial.

SAMPLE DEMO TRADE # 1:

Let us execute a sample trade on the OANDA® platform. I will short GBP against the US dollar for this trade. The rationale for this trade is as follows:

- British economy has still not fully recovered from the financial downturn that impacted the global economies since late 2007. The GDP and retail sales remain weak while the US economy has since stabilized and is showing signs of growth. Therefore fundamentally it seems a sound trade.

- The GBP/USD pair has been channeling between Resistance at 1.6277 and Support at 1.5327 since November 2010. Lately the pair has broken through this channel to the downside and is currently trading at 1.5030. Therefore our planned trade is also supported technically.

- We can either enter the trade at current levels or wait for the price to retrace back to its previous support at 1.5327 and then open our short trade thereby giving us a better entry level. Please note that the previous support should now serve as resistance and if the price holds at 1.5327 then it further confirms that we have a trade with a higher probability of success. It is also important to note that there is still no guarantee that even after stacking all the factors in our favor the trade will end up being a successful trade. I am going to address this issue in detail in Chapter 7.

- I am confident with our set up and am ready to sell the GBP/USD pair at current levels.

- From the GBP/USD chart below you can see that the width of the channel which is broken by price action to the downside was 950 pips therefore our Take Profit level will be equal to 950 pips from the previous support. This profit target is calculated as $1.5227 - 950 = 1.4277$, therefore we will keep our profit target at around a round number 1.4300 (thick yellow line on the chart below)

- We will place our protective stop within the channel at around 1.5477, therefore if the trade goes against us then we are looking at a 450 pip loss, but if our trade is successful then we will net around 700 pips. This gives us roughly a favorable 2:1 win loss ratio.

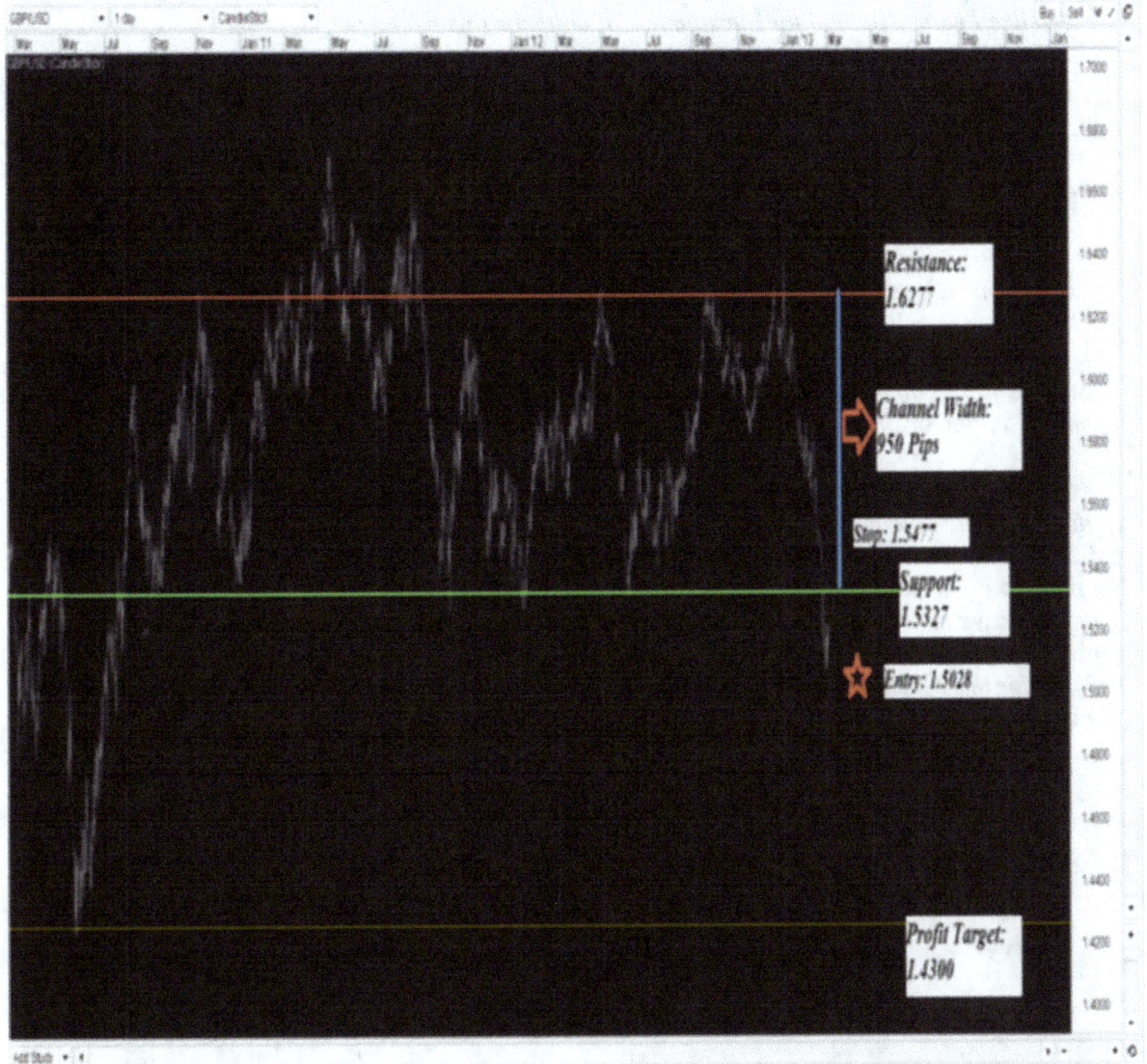

- To execute the short GBP/USD trade, click on the GBP/USD price quote on the quote list.
- This open a new "Market order window"
- Click on "Market Order'
- Click on "Sell"
- Enter the number of units to be traded. As our account has $ 100,000 therefore I will trade 1 mini-lot i.e. 10,000 units of GBP/USD. This is a demo trade therefore I am not going to open another trade till either this trade is stopped out for a loss or it hits our profit target, therefore keeping our stop & take profit levels in mind I am going to risk 3-5% of our capital on this trade. This risk allows me to open approximately 15 mini-lots or 1.5 lots (150,000 units), but for simplicity sake I am going to sell I lot (100,000 units) of GBP/USD.

- Hence I enter 100,000 for our number of units for this trade
- We got an entry price of 1.5032
- I adjusted our "stop loss" from 1.5477 to 1.5400 to get a better risk and reward ratio.
- Next I enter the "Take profit" level at 1.4300
- For one mini-lot (10,000 units) the price/pip is $1 therefore for 10 mini-lots or 1 lot (100,000 units) the price/pip is $10.

- Take Profit & Stop Loss values are automatically calculated for you. If our trade is successful and it reaches our take profit level then we will gain 732 pips (entry level 1.5032 – take profit level 1.4300 = 732 pips). As each pip is equal to $10 for this trade therefore our profit will be $ 7320.
- On the other hand if the trade goes against us and hits our stop loss then we set to lose 368 pips (Stop level 1.5400 – entry level 1.5032 = 368 pips). As each pip is equal to $ 10 for this trade therefore our loss will be $ 3680 or about 3.5 % of our capital.

- We are using $ 7516 as a margin for this trade which is about 7.5% of our capital. The margin is automatically calculated for us, but for education purposes as the current rate of GBP/USD is roughly 1.50 that means that 1 Pound equals 1.50 US dollars therefore in order to sell 100,000 units of GB pounds I need to put aside 150,000 US dollars if 1:1 leverage is used, but due to advantage of leverage trading in Forex we can trade these lots by setting aside a smaller margin. Our demo platform is set at 20:1 leverage and I have not changed it to 50:1, therefore we are required to set aside only (150,000/20 = $ 7500) for this trade. If you want to change the leverage to 50:1 then go to "Account" and Click on "Change leverage". Remember in USA the maximum leverage allowed is 50:1.

Click "Submit" and your trade is up and running.
The open trade will then show up on your "Trade" window

We don't have to monitor it on a minute to minute basis. Our work is done; I will just visit our platform once every other day to see how the trade is progressing. Easy job; isn't it!

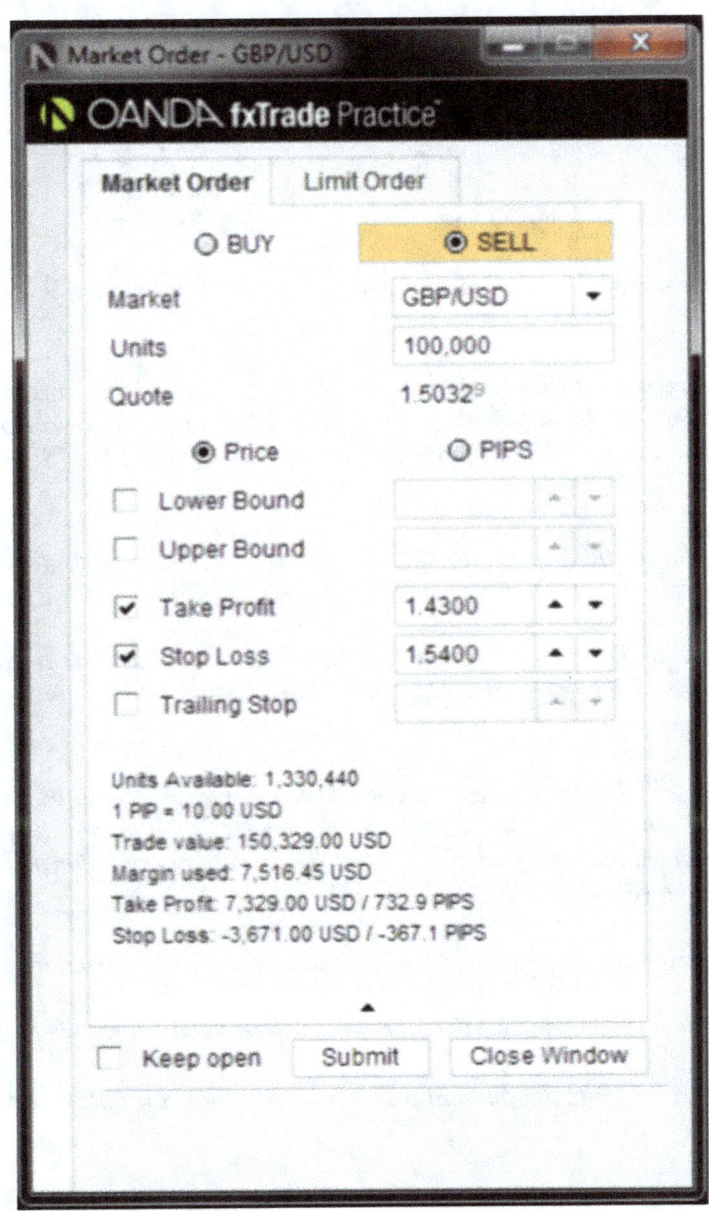

I have promised earlier that once we have our demo trade up and running then I will revisit the "Account Summary" section and explain to you its various components. Let us review that section before we call it a day for today.

Account Summary (USD)	
Balance	100,001.92
Unrealized P&L	10.00
Unrealized P&L (%)	0.01
Net Asset Value	100,011.92
Margin Alert	7,514.90
Realized P&L	0.00
Margin Used	7,514.90
Margin Available	92,497.02
Margin Closeout Value	100,022.42
Margin Closeout Percent (%)	3.76
Position Value	150,298.00

"Balance" represents our starting balance of 100,001.92. We have gained $ 1.92 due to daily interest on our deposit over the last week period.

"Unrealized P & L" represents the Profit or Loss of our open positions. This profit or Loss stays unrealized till the time the open trades are closed. The price of GBP/USD has moved down 1 pip from 1.5032 to 1.5031, as each pip for this trade equates to $ 10 therefore we currently have a profit of $ 10 which shows as our current Unrealized Profit.

Our $10 profit is equal to 0.01% of our total deposit of 100,001.92 therefore this percentage appears as "Unrealized Profit" in percentage of the account.

Add $ 10 to our initial deposit of $100,001.92 therefore currently our account's "Net Asset Value" is 100,011.92. All these figures will keep on changing on a second to second basis as the price of GBP/USD fluctuates with each tic.

Margin Alert is set at $ 7514.90 that means we have to be negative 9200 pips on our trade for this alert to go into effect. This alert will only occur if we did not use the protective stop and the price of GBP/USD moved up approximately 9200 pips from our entry price to 2.4232. This is not possible for this trade because our trade will be stopped out at our stop level of 1.5400.

"Realized P& L" represents the profit or loss accumulated from the closed trades.

We are using a 20:1 leverage therefore the margin required for this trade is $ 7514, as explained earlier.

"Margin Available" represents the amount that our open trade can utilize or we can utilize this amount to open other trades.

"Margin Closeout Value is the net asset value plus the unrealized profit & loss.

"Margin Close out percent "is half the margin percentage of the account, e.g. the margin used for this trade is $ 7514 which is approximately 7.5% of the account, therefore one half of 7.5 is 3.75 which represents the margin closeout percent. In simple words it means that if you are not using a protective stop for this trade and the trade gets negative $ 96,250 or negative 9625 pips then you will receive a margin call and your trade will be automatically closed and the remaining balance in your account will stand at only $ 3750.

"Position Value" is the amount of money required to trade 100,000 units of GBP/USD without 20:1 leverage. This clearly demonstrates that it would not be possible for regular traders to trade such large units of a currency pair without leverage in the Forex market. Leverage has its advantages in addition to the risks associated with it.

The GBP/USD reached 1.5400 level today, April 11th 2013, at around 6:00 am and hit our stop loss therefore we were stopped out of this trade with a loss of $3680.

SAMPLE DEMO TRADE # 2:

Next I am going to demonstrate placing a second demo trade on our demo platform; I'll also explain the rationale behind this trade. The steps are exactly the same for placing a trade with real money on a real trading account. I am going to select NZD/JPY as our currency pair for this trade and go long this pair, which actually means that we are going to buy the NZ dollars and sell the Japanese Yen. Currently Yen has been weakening while the New Zealand (NZ) economy has been stabilizing since the worldwide economic crisis of 2007 and we have bullish statements coming out of their Central Bank.

In addition, if you remember that early on in this chapter I mentioned that, the NZD Reserve Bank offers an interest rate of 2.50% on your deposits while the interest rates in Japan are below 0.1%. This interest rate differential makes the NZD dollar more attractive to the investors who are seeking a higher rate of return on their investment. Smart Joe raises a very pertinent question that if the rationale behind this trade is the interest rate differential, then why not go long the AUD/JPY pair rather than NZD/JPY, because Australian Reserve Bank offers a return of 3% on deposits. Great question Joe, really a smart question; Ms. Sarah annoyingly states that this was also her question. Calm down guys, here is the answer. Lately Australian economy has been cooling off a bit due to the slowing of the Chinese economy. China is Australia's main trading partner and a sluggish Chinese economy has a negative impact on the Australian economy. Due to this impact the Reserve Bank of Australia has indicated a cut in their interest rates over the next few months, these cuts will narrow the interest rate differential between the Japanese and Australian currencies therefore the AUD is going to lose its appeal, and hence I choose the NZD/JPY pair.

The process of borrowing money from an economy with an extremely low interest rate and then buying and holding the currency with a much higher interest rate is called a <u>Carry Trade</u>. During stable economic times the carry trade seems to work well as the currency with a higher interest rate keeps on appreciating, but during periods of uncertainty the carry trade unwinds as investors sell riskier assets (assets with high interest rates like AUD, NZD etc.) and tend to move into safe haven currencies like Swiss Franc, US Dollar and Japanese Yen. This was the exact reason why the Yen, Dollar and the Franc significantly appreciated since 2007.

Disclaimer: *The content on this page is for educational purposes only and should not be construed in any way as trading advice. The risk of loss in online trading of stocks, Forex, options, and foreign equities is substantial.*

When I open a long NZD/JPY trade, I am hoping that the pair will move up from the current 79.12 levels so that I can earn positive Pips and profit from this trade and in addition if I hold this trade for a longer period I will be paid an interest by my broker on a daily basis. If on the other hand I short NZD/JPY pair then I will be paying my broker an interest from my account on a daily basis. The interest is paid to your account or deducted from your account daily at 5:00 pm EST by majority of the brokers. Oanda ® pays or deducts interest on your positions in a slightly different format. If you even open a position at 4:59 pm EST you will still receive or pay the interest at 5:00 pm EST and will reflect on your account may be a few hours later. On Wednesday you either receive or pay triple the amount of interest because it includes interests for Saturday and Sunday, as the market is closed on the weekend and the accounts are not credited or debited during the period the market is closed. Oanda ® pays or deducts interest on a daily basis, which includes Saturday and Sunday therefore the interest does not triplicate on Wednesday.

The illustration below shows what pairs pay interest when you buy or sell them and on which pairs you have to pay interest if you go long or short. In addition the example also lists the current Buy and Sell rates, Margin Requirements, Spread and the Pip cost of that pair.

Symbol	Spread	Roll Sell	Roll Buy	Pip Cost	MMR
EUR/USD	2.4	0.03	-0.14	0.10	30
USD/JPY	2.5	-0.06	0.03	0.11	20
GBP/USD	2.4	-0.12	0.06	0.10	36
USD/CHF	2.6	-0.12	0.05	0.11	20
AUD/USD	2.1	-1.11	0.54	0.10	24
NZD/USD	2.5	-0.77	0.36	0.10	20
EUR/GBP	2.0	0.08	-0.25	0.16	30
GBP/CAD	4.0	0.14	-0.33	0.10	36
EUR/AUD	3.0	0.73	-1.51	0.10	30

Roll Sell represents the interest/micro-lot/day if you go short that pair, Roll Buy represents the interest/micro-lot/day if you go long that pair,(if the figure is negative then you pay a daily interest for that pair and if the figure is positive then you receive the interest in your account, this is also referred to as **negative and positive daily Swap/Roll-over respectively**), and MMR represents the minimum margin requirement/ micro-lot for that pair.

Disclaimer: The content on this page is for educational purposes only and should not be construed in any way as trading advice. The risk of loss in online trading of stocks, Forex, options, and foreign equities is substantial.

Let us determine how many units of NZD/JPY we are going to buy for this demo trade.

Let us assume that we have $ 50,000 in our demo account, therefore we are going to buy 5000 units (5 micro-lots) of NZD/JPY (refer to chapter 3, section on lots)

Currently the NZD/JPY exchange rate is 79.12 that means 1 NZ dollar equals 79.12 Yens

To buy 5000 units of NZD we need 79.12 × 5000 = 396000 Yens to exchange.

As our demo account is in US dollars for this transaction we need to change our Yens to USD first and then purchase NZD's; this will require $ 4235 because currently 93.5 Yens equal 1 US Dollar (396000 / 93.5 = 4235)

As Forex trading is a leveraged market and the current leverage allowed in USA is 50:1 therefore we only need around $ 85 instead of $4235,(4235/50 = 84.7), to be set aside as margin to open this position.

Therefore you can hold 5000 NZ dollars by offering only $ 85 as a margin on your platform, but if you went to the exchange counter you have to approximately bring 396000 Yens or approximately 4235 US dollars to buy 5000 NZ dollars.

Now we have converted our Yens to USD's first & then NZ dollars therefore 1 pip move on NZD/JPY for one micro-lot will equal 0.11 dollars (or 11 cents)

We do not have any other trade open on our platform therefore we can risk 10% ($5000) of our capital on this trade.

This allows us to open 250 micro-lots for our $ 5000 margin (5 micro-lots for $ 85, 50 micro-lots for $ 850 and 250 micro-lots for $ 4250). We could have opened 294 micro-lots for NZD/JPY for $ 5000 margin but to keep the calculations simple we opened 250 micro-lots.

You must be getting tired or even confused with these calculations but don't worry these are for educational purposes only, the trading station displays all these figures and you don't have to focus on specific calculations. Your focus should now only be on opening 250 micro-lots of NZD/JPY.

> *Log-in to your trading platform we set up earlier.*
> *Create Market Order for NZD/JPY exactly like we did earlier for GBP/USD demo trade. This means that we are buying the NZD/JPY at the current market price which is 79.23*

We buy 250 micro-lots as discussed earlier. The margin we set aside for the trade is automatically calculated for you ($ 4250). Pip cost/250 micro-lots are also calculated (which is .11 dollars /micro-lot and therefore 26.62 dollars/250 micro-lots). We brought this pair at current market price of 79.23. Always leave the Time in Force as "GTC" that means good till closed. We have checked the "Stop" level and inserted a rate of 78.23. This means that if the trade goes against us we will have the trade close automatically at 100 pips from our open price we got which was 79.23. We also checked the Limit box and inserted a rate of 82.23, (300 pips from our entry) which means that if the trade goes in our favor and the exchange rate of NZD/JPY reaches 82.23 then the trade will automatically close giving us a profit of 300 pips. Then Click OK and you now have an open trade.

The advantage of checking the Stop and Limit boxes is that you don't have to continuously monitor your trade. You can close the trading platform and carry on with your activities and the trade is automatically managed. The trade will be closed out when it hits one of your set levels. It could be your stop level first. It has happened many times that the trade initially goes against you, hits your stop level thereby causing you a loss and then moving in your intended direction and reaching your profit level, but you would have already been closed out therefore your trade can't profit. You only profit if your trade is open and the exchange level reaches your profit target rate.

If this trade hits our stop then we will lose 100 pips as pip rate / 250 micro-lots is 26.62 a 100 pip loss will create a final loss of $26.62 \times 100 = \$ 2662$

If this trade does not reach our stop loss first and reaches our profit target then we will gain 300 pips and as pip rate / 250 micro-lots is 26.62 a 300 pip profit will create a final profit of $26.62 \times 300 = \$ 7986$, handsome profit from one trade.

In addition for each day we hold this trade we get a profit of 0.39 dollars / micro-lot, and as we have bought 250 micro-lots, the daily interest on this pair credited to our account at 5:00 pm EST will be $ 97.5 & if our trade stays open for 10 days we will earn $ 975 as interest on this trade. I have opened this demo trade on 2/17/2013 & will wait for it to close automatically and then will analyze the results of this trade.

Today is Wednesday 2/20/2013 and our trade went against us and hit our stop loss therefore we suffered a loss. It is time to analyze the NZD/JPY trade.

We based our trade on the Fundamental principles, as the NZ dollar offers a higher interest rate and the Japanese yen has been weakening over the last couple of months.

Did we look into the technical picture and determine the support or resistance levels or any price patterns? **NO**

Should we have looked at the technical chart before entering the trade? **Would have helped**

By combining the Fundamental and Technical analysis could we have guaranteed a successful trade? **There is a possibility that we might have had a better outcome but the success of the trade could not have been guaranteed, even by an expert trader.**

One thing I know for a fact is that Mr. Wheeler, the governor of the Reserve Bank of New Zealand in his speech on Tuesday evening (Wednesday morning in NZ) painted a dismal picture about New Zealand manufacturing sector which lead to a drop in the value of NZ dollar and that definitely had a negative impact on our NZD/JPY trade. This is one of the reasons I have mentioned in the earlier sections of these chapters that it is important to pay attention to the Central Bank Governors/Chairmen comments as these comments often move the market. Some excerpts from his speech are as follows:

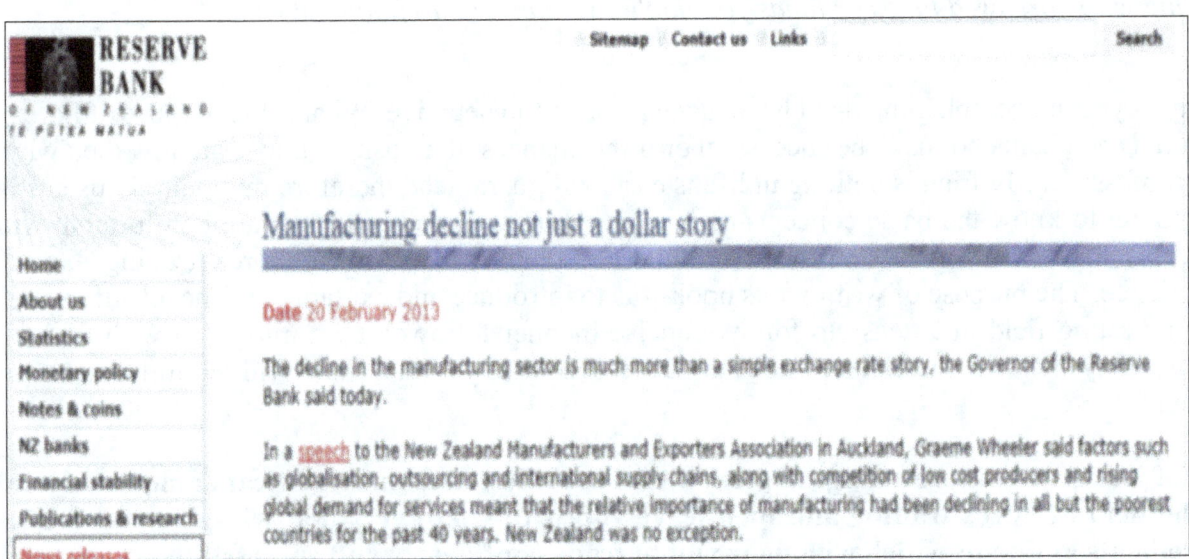

Disclaimer: The content on this page is for educational purposes only and should not be construed in any way as trading advice. The risk of loss in online trading of stocks, Forex, options, and foreign equities is substantial.

As our stop was placed at 100 pips from entry therefore we suffered a 100 pip loss which equates to $2669.54 (100 × 26.62 {pip rate for 250 micro-lots or $ 0.11/pip})

As we were long NZD/JPY therefore we earned an interest of $ 19.50 for the two days the trade was on

Therefore Total Loss = Trade Loss + Interest = $ - 2669.54 + $ 19.50 = $ - 2650.04

This accounts to about 5% of our account loss as we assumed we had $ 50,000 in our demo account before opening this trade.

As this is virtual-money the loss does not bother us but if it was your real account then you would be pretty upset with the market. Your emotions will be high and your confidence would be shaken for the next trade.

The next trade might be more difficult because you are looking forward to a trade that would recoup your previous trade losses and also to bring some handsome profits to your account, which will allow your account to grow.

There is no guarantee that your next trade will be successful. You might have 6-8 or more straight losses that will significantly drain your account. This is one of the reasons majority of traders fail because their emotions take over, and they make a lot of irrational trades in order to quickly gain profits which in the end leads to multiple losses, a shrinking account and finally a margin call. Now you have to re-fund your account if you want to continue trading. Trading can be very addictive and trading with borrowed funds or funds you don't own can lead to financial ruin.

Many of you are complaining that I have made it sound too negative. What is the purpose of Forex trading if there is no chance for us to be successful or if the chances of a positive trades are low then why pursue this profession. My friends nothing in life is easy and guaranteed therefore my main focus has been for you to get to know the basic concepts of Forex trading well and once you are comfortable with these concepts then with your smartness, readiness and knowledge make Forex trading a worthwhile experience. The purpose of writing this book was to introduce and explain the concepts of this relatively new investing field in an easy to follow concise manner followed by arming you with tools that will significantly increase the chances of your success, so that you can trade with confidence on your live account.

The objectives of the preceding chapters was to provide you with a significant amount of knowledge in the field of Forex trading and then leave you with <u>Chapter 7</u> that will give you the required ingredients and tools which will allow you to trade confidently and successfully.

Your trading stations allow you to run your activity report on a daily, weekly, monthly or yearly basis to review your overall results? The yearly report also helps you determine your annual profit or loss for tax purposes. I am not a tax consultant therefore you have to talk to a CPA to discuss your tax obligations from Forex income.

This is our second loss in a row, the NZD/JPY trade we put on was based upon fundamental factors and the GBP/USD trade was technically sound as the GBP/USD pair broke out of a well-defined channel to the downside and we had entered short in anticipation that the GBP/USD pair will continue to depreciate. Unfortunately this is the reality of Forex that in-spite of a strong fundamental or technical signal there is no guarantee that the trade will be successful, and there is a possibility that you might end up with a string of losses in a row which can deplete your trading account. This is the very reason a majority of Forex traders get discouraged and unsuccessfully quit Forex trading. Unless there is major shift in trading philosophy, the majority of Forex traders will continue to encounter failure. My work defies these old standards of Forex teachings and is presented in chapter seven.

The next chapter is the soul of my book; it is the epitome of hard work that I have put in studying the Forex markets over the last seven years. I came to realize that in order to be consistently successful you have to deviate from the regular run of the mill coaching and training being provided to the newbies in Forex trading. You have to challenge the current hard core concepts and cut down on the noise being generated by the trading pundits, because these same concepts are responsible for above 95% failure rate in Forex trading.

My aim is to introduce new ideas and concepts which reduce risk, make sense, are easily reproducible and make your Forex experience worthwhile. That is enough of preaching for today, and now back over to teaching with chapter VII

KEY TO SUCCESS

CHAPTER SEVEN

KEY TO SUCCESS

In the previous chapter we took our first steps towards practically trading Forex, opened a couple of demo accounts, familiarized ourselves with the trading platforms and finally took some sample trades. We have learned from the earlier chapters that following the fundamental and technical principles do not guarantee a successful trade; there are possibilities of multiple losses even if the analysis presents us with the low risk trades. Therefore in this chapter I present a trading strategy that reduces the risk, is effective and above all is reproducible time and time again.

It is now time to open a live Forex trading account and start experiencing the exciting and intriguing world of Forex investing. I will leave the choice of selecting the broker to you. The application process is simple, you are required to complete a detailed application online and provide some pertinent documents for a real account. It might take a couple of days for your application to be approved. Upon approval you can fund your live account with a credit card or a wire transfer. My personal criteria for selecting a broker are as follows:

- Is regulated
- Is transparent
- Maintains adequate reserves
- Allows the trader to choose the leverage
- Allows the ability to trade anywhere from 1 unit to 100,000 units (full lot)
- Allows sub-accounts within a main trading account
- Easy to use trading platform

Before we start trading our live accounts we should have clear expectations of the outcomes for Forex investing. A number of individuals use Forex trading as a tool to overnight riches. They expect to turn a $100 into a million dollars by trading Forex. I don't blame these individuals but unfortunately this is how the so called experts have presented Forex to the newbies. I am not going to spend my time here countering these claims but I know for a fact that if the failure rate is extremely high then there is definitely something wrong with the method of trading being propagated. This very reason motivated me to reject standard teachings in Forex and study these markets so that I can achieve the results that meet my expectations.

Expectations:

- Control risk by proper position sizing
- Attain success rates in excess of 90%
- Achieve returns comparable or higher than the standard financial vehicles available
- Limit time spent in front of the computer on trading stations.

Disclaimer: The content on this page is for educational purposes only and should not be construed in any way as trading advice. The risk of loss in online trading of stocks, Forex, options, and foreign equities is substantial.

To substantiate my method I listed a Forex trading system on a public forum and would like to share the results of this virtual system as a prelude to describing my trading strategy.

Beginning Account Value (March 2010)	$100,000.00
Number of Trades Entered	358
Closed Trades	346
Success Rate for Closed Trades	346/346 Positive = 100%
Gross Value (March 2013)	$149,941.00
Rate of Return on Closed Trades	16.64% / annum
Open Trades	12
Current Value of Open Trades (March 2013)	-$7,322.00
Risk on Open Trades	4.88%
Net Value (March 2013)	$142,619.00

Remember there is a substantial risk of loss in trading. Past performance is not indicative of future results. Do not trade with money you cannot afford to lose

The results of this virtual system represent a reasonable rate of return with less than 5% risk on open trades. I use open trades as a way of investment in the market and then wait for these trades to turn positive which are then harvested upon reaching a set level of positive return. A screen shot of some positive closed trades is exhibited on the following pages:

Hypothetical Trading Results								
Opened ET	B/S	#	Symbol	Price	Closed	Price	Risk	P/L
3/19/13 22:13	BUY	1	AUD/JPY	98.551	3/20 23:37	99.579	Low	$106
1/25/13 6:49	BUY	1	CAD/CHF	0.92015	3/14 8:34	0.93203	Low	$123
3/7/13 22:07	BUY	1	EUR/JPY	124.873	3/11 22:53	125.861	Low	$101
2/3/13 18:50	BUY	2	EUR/JPY	124.071	3/7 22:07	124.845	Low	$160
2/25/13 22:23	BUY	1	CAD/JPY	90.197	3/7 7:10	91.344	Low	$121
2/25/13 22:24	BUY	1	USD/JPY	92.426	3/4 22:26	93.199	Low	$82
2/26/13 22:20	BUY	1	AUD/JPY	94.028	2/27 21:52	94.937	Low	$97
1/30/13 22:12	BUY	1	AUD/CHF	0.94695	2/19 7:51	0.95536	Low	$90
2/7/13 8:44	BUY	1	NZD/JPY	78.163	2/13 23:02	79.219	Low	$112
2/8/13 7:45	BUY	1	CAD/JPY	92.506	2/11 19:41	93.679	Low	$123
2/3/13 18:51	BUY	1	CAD/JPY	93.132	2/7 6:56	94.315	Low	$125
2/4/13 19:34	BUY	1	NZD/JPY	77.828	2/6 7:38	78.882	Low	$112
1/31/13 20:42	BUY	1	GBP/JPY	145.596	2/5 7:46	147.079	Low	$158
1/31/13 20:43	BUY	1	USD/JPY	91.795	2/3 18:51	92.814	Low	$109
1/31/13 20:42	BUY	1	EUR/JPY	124.958	2/1 6:50	125.723	Low	$82
1/25/13 6:49	BUY	1	AUD/JPY	94.931	2/1 6:49	95.675	Low	$80
1/25/13 6:49	BUY	1	CAD/JPY	90.515	1/31 20:41	92.015	Low	$162
1/28/13 6:45	BUY	1	NZD/JPY	75.178	1/28 21:53	75.929	Low	$82
11/18/12 18:27	BUY	1	USD/CAD	1.00082	1/27/13 21:20	1.00778	Low	$68
1/17/13 9:09	BUY	1	USD/JPY	89.386	1/25 6:48	90.866	Low	$162
1/21/13 22:04	BUY	1	GBP/JPY	141.589	1/25 6:48	143.413	Low	$200

Disclaimer: The content on this page is for educational purposes only and should not be construed in any way as trading advice. The risk of loss in online trading of stocks, Forex, options, and foreign equities is substantial.

1/21/13 22:03	BUY	1 EUR/JPY	118.996	1/25 6:47	122.067	Low	$337
1/14/13 21:55	BUY	1 EUR/JPY	119.324	1/18 7:51	120.196	Low	$96
4/5/11 21:47	BUY	5 EUR/CHF	1.24873	1/17/13 20:57	1.25060	Normal	$95
1/15/13 7:49	BUY	1 GBP/JPY	141.876	1/17 9:08	142.892	Low	$113
12/16/12 17:42	BUY	1 CAD/CHF	0.93059	1/14/13 21:53	0.93918	Low	$92
1/11/13 7:51	BUY	1 EUR/JPY	118.066	1/13 17:34	119.737	Low	$185
1/1/13 23:20	BUY	1 GBP/JPY	142.481	1/10 23:16	143.760	Low	$143
1/8/13 7:46	BUY	1 USD/JPY	87.520	1/10 23:16	89.022	Low	$168
1/8/13 7:44	BUY	1 CAD/JPY	88.835	1/10 23:15	90.527	Low	$189
1/1/13 23:20	BUY	1 NZD/JPY	72.912	1/10 7:08	74.310	Low	$157
1/1/13 23:20	BUY	1 AUD/JPY	91.302	1/6 22:00	92.317	Low	$114
12/19/12 16:38	BUY	1 AUD/CHF	0.95696	1/3/13 7:01	0.96913	Low	$131
12/31/12 7:39	BUY	1 USD/JPY	86.179	1/1/13 23:19	87.166	Low	$112
12/27/12 22:35	BUY	1 EUR/JPY	114.488	1/1/13 23:19	115.671	Low	$135
12/27/12 22:34	BUY	1 GBP/JPY	139.313	12/31 10:12	140.213	Low	$103
12/19/12 16:37	BUY	1 CHF/JPY	92.518	12/27 22:32	94.685	Low	$250
12/12/12 22:44	BUY	1 AUD/JPY	88.214	12/27 22:31	89.636	Low	$164
12/21/12 7:43	BUY	1 NZD/JPY	69.305	12/27 22:31	70.928	Low	$187
5/5/10 14:28	BUY	5 USD/JPY	84.827	12/27/12 22:30	86.434	High	$925
12/16/12 17:42	BUY	1 GBP/JPY	136.231	12/19 16:37	137.141	Low	$107
12/12/12 20:22	BUY	1 NZD/JPY	70.323	12/16 17:42	71.219	Low	$105
12/12/12 22:44	BUY	1 EUR/JPY	109.337	12/16 17:22	110.616	Low	$151
12/12/12 7:46	BUY	1 GBP/JPY	133.873	12/12 22:43	134.896	Low	$121

Disclaimer: The content on this page is for educational purposes only and should not be construed in any way as trading advice. The risk of loss in online trading of stocks, Forex, options, and foreign equities is substantial.

11/29/12 22:07	BUY	1	CHF/JPY	88.949	12/12 20:21	89.976	Low	$122
12/11/12 7:49	BUY	1	AUD/JPY	86.542	12/12 7:45	87.444	Low	$108
12/11/12 7:49	BUY	1	EUR/JPY	107.124	12/12 7:44	108.158	Low	$124
11/23/12 10:42	BUY	1	CAD/JPY	82.826	12/9 18:19	83.600	Low	$93
11/29/12 22:07	BUY	1	AUD/CHF	0.96630	12/6 21:43	0.97684	Low	$112
11/23/12 10:42	BUY	1	GBP/JPY	131.742	12/4 22:32	132.547	Low	$97
11/23/12 8:36	BUY	1	EUR/JPY	106.228	11/29 22:06	107.109	Low	$106
11/18/12 18:13	BUY	1	NZD/USD	0.81327	11/23 10:41	0.82249	Low	$91
11/20/12 21:17	BUY	1	NZD/JPY	66.861	11/23 10:40	67.725	Low	$104
11/18/12 18:04	BUY	1	GBP/JPY	129.365	11/20 21:17	130.445	Low	$131
11/15/12 7:52	BUY	1	CHF/JPY	86.096	11/20 21:17	87.101	Low	$122
10/23/12 22:31	BUY	1	EUR/JPY	103.719	11/20 21:16	104.944	Low	$149
11/5/12 7:46	BUY	1	CAD/JPY	80.523	11/18 18:14	81.320	Low	$97
3/20/12 22:44	BUY	2	GBP/JPY	129.019	11/18 18:03	129.330	Low	$74
11/9/12 6:49	BUY	1	NZD/JPY	64.585	11/15 7:51	65.926	Low	$164
11/2/12 6:48	BUY	1	CAD/CHF	0.93931	11/5 7:45	0.94708	Low	$81
9/14/12 6:52	BUY	1	AUD/JPY	82.626	11/2 6:47	83.284	Low	$81
10/19/12 7:37	BUY	2	CAD/CHF	0.93488	11/2 6:47	0.93891	Low	$84
9/17/12 22:20	BUY	1	NZD/JPY	64.975	10/25 7:49	65.998	Low	$127
10/16/12 19:28	SELL	1	EUR/GBP	0.81340	10/25 7:49	0.80539	Low	$128
10/5/12 7:48	BUY	1	AUD/CHF	0.95507	10/24 6:53	0.96510	Low	$106
10/19/12 7:37	BUY	1	EUR/JPY	103.342	10/22 19:12	104.428	Low	$135
9/6/12 19:48	BUY	1	CAD/JPY	80.299	10/17	81.003	Low	$88

Disclaimer: The content on this page is for educational purposes only and should not be construed in any way as trading advice. The risk of loss in online trading of stocks, Forex, options, and foreign equities is substantial.

10/16/12 19:29	BUY	1 CAD/CHF	0.93505	10/17 22:31	0.94397	Low	$96
9/19/12 7:42	BUY	1 EUR/USD	1.30186	10/16 22:26	1.31154	Low	$96
9/14/12 6:52	BUY	1 EUR/JPY	102.125	10/16 19:28	103.371	Low	$157
10/5/12 7:48	BUY	1 CAD/CHF	0.95022	10/16 19:27	0.95915	Low	$95
9/14/12 6:52	BUY	1 CHF/JPY	83.855	10/8 22:44	84.770	Low	$115
6/21/12 7:29	BUY	1 NZD/JPY	63.929	9/17 22:19	65.037	Low	$141
4/30/12 18:06	BUY	2 EUR/JPY	101.597	9/14 6:51	102.121	Low	$132
5/8/12 22:16	BUY	2 CHF/JPY	83.155	9/14 6:51	83.860	Low	$179
9/3/12 10:35	BUY	1 AUD/CHF	0.97751	9/14 6:50	0.98760	Low	$105
4/24/12 7:53	BUY	2 CAD/JPY	79.931	9/7 7:51	80.258	Low	$81
8/8/12 8:45	BUY	1 GBP/CHF	1.52342	9/6 19:47	1.53174	Low	$84
7/31/12 8:38	BUY	1 CAD/CHF	0.97447	8/15 23:41	0.98815	Low	$139
7/23/12 6:07	BUY	1 AUD/CHF	1.01971	8/15 23:39	1.02735	Low	$77
7/2/12 22:29	BUY	1 AUD/USD	1.02678	7/31 8:38	1.05132	Low	$244
7/12/12 22:24	BUY	1 CAD/CHF	0.96635	7/31 8:38	0.97495	Low	$86
6/18/12 22:21	BUY	1 GBP/CHF	1.49499	7/23 6:06	1.51927	Low	$246
3/20/12 7:50	BUY	2 AUD/USD	1.02302	7/12 22:23	1.02652	Low	$68
5/8/12 22:18	BUY	1 AUD/JPY	80.445	7/2 22:29	81.401	Low	$118
3/26/12 20:02	BUY	3 NZD/JPY	63.571	6/21 7:28	63.877	Low	$112
5/28/12 10:08	BUY	2 GBP/CHF	1.49055	6/21 7:28	1.49450	Low	$81
6/17/12 18:20	SELL	1 EUR/GBP	0.81007	6/18 22:19	0.80355	Low	$101
5/16/12 7:56	BUY	1 NZD/USD	0.76687	6/18 22:16	0.77554	Low	$86
				6/10 19:22			

Disclaimer: *The content on this page is for educational purposes only and should not be construed in any way as trading advice. The risk of loss in online trading of stocks, Forex, options, and foreign equities is substantial.*

5/16/12 7:55	BUY	1 NZD/CHF	0.72360	6/6 22:07	0.73615	Low	$130
5/8/12 22:15	BUY	1 AUD/CAD	1.00785	6/6 22:06	1.02271	Low	$144
5/14/12 20:41	BUY	2 GBP/CHF	1.49979	5/28 10:07	1.50423	Low	$91
5/16/12 7:56	BUY	1 NZD/CAD	0.77321	5/28 10:05	0.78088	Low	$74
5/20/12 17:37	BUY	1 CAD/CHF	0.92008	5/23 21:19	0.93115	Low	$115
8/5/10 8:46	BUY	5 GBP/CHF	1.50230	5/14/12 20:40	1.50623	Normal	$205
4/5/12 7:13	BUY	1 EUR/JPY	107.084	4/20 6:59	107.816	Low	$89
4/10/12 7:46	BUY	1 CAD/JPY	81.280	4/17 22:16	82.115	Low	$102
3/20/12 22:47	BUY	1 NZD/CHF	0.74594	4/12 21:04	0.75672	Low	$117
4/3/12 23:09	BUY	1 AUD/CAD	1.02018	4/9 22:04	1.02921	Low	$90
3/23/12 7:50	BUY	1 CAD/CHF	0.90866	4/3 23:09	0.91932	Low	$116
3/22/12 22:42	BUY	1 CAD/JPY	82.946	3/26 20:02	83.673	Low	$87
10/30/11 22:37	BUY	1 CHF/JPY	91.319	3/20/12 22:45	92.001	Low	$81
2/26/12 17:29	BUY	1 EUR/JPY	109.736	3/20 22:44	111.005	Low	$151
3/14/12 7:00	BUY	1 AUD/USD	1.04840	3/18 18:00	1.05892	Low	$104
3/9/12 10:45	BUY	1 CAD/JPY	83.365	3/14 6:58	84.204	Low	$100
2/26/12 17:29	BUY	1 GBP/JPY	129.416	3/13 19:56	130.235	Low	$98
1/20/12 7:06	BUY	1 CAD/CHF	0.92206	3/13 16:37	0.93328	Low	$121
4/10/11 20:41	BUY	5 CAD/JPY	83.077	3/9/12 10:45	83.366	Normal	$170
2/24/12 7:53	SELL	1 EUR/GBP	0.84862	2/29 21:02	0.83766	Low	$173
2/26/12 17:28	BUY	1 NZD/CHF	0.74903	2/29 7:04	0.75762	Low	$95
8/4/11 6:14	BUY	2 GBP/JPY	127.162	2/26/12 17:28	129.420	Low	$552
5/5/11 22:43	BUY	3 EUR/JPY	108.252	2/26/12	109.692	Normal	$527

Disclaimer: The content on this page is for educational purposes only and should not be construed in any way as trading advice. The risk of loss in online trading of stocks, Forex, options, and foreign equities is substantial.

1/29/12 20:58	BUY	1	NZD/JPY	63.015	2/5 17:28 19:19	63.791	Low	$100
1/20/12 7:05	BUY	1	NZD/JPY	61.949	1/25 20:53	63.561	Low	$206
1/8/12 19:37	BUY	1	GBP/USD	1.54015	1/22 18:45	1.55455	Low	$143
10/30/11 21:40	BUY	2	NZD/JPY	61.619	1/20/12 7:04	61.924	Low	$77
12/29/11 10:47	BUY	1	CAD/CHF	0.92303	1/11/12 6:48	0.93840	Low	$160
1/8/12 19:36	BUY	1	AUD/USD	1.01580	1/9 23:02	1.03012	Low	$142
1/8/12 19:36	BUY	1	NZD/USD	0.77843	1/9 23:02	0.79377	Low	$152
12/2/11 7:56	BUY	1	AUD/USD	1.02885	1/3/12 6:50	1.03623	Low	$73
12/29/11 10:47	BUY	1	GBP/USD	1.54159	12/30 9:02	1.55169	Low	$100
4/1/11 9:36	BUY	3	CAD/CHF	0.91865	12/29 10:46	0.92230	Low	$113
12/8/11 23:05	BUY	1	NZD/CHF	0.71145	12/22 7:15	0.72292	Low	$121
12/13/11 23:04	BUY	1	NZD/USD	0.75679	12/20 20:08	0.76939	Low	$125
12/13/11 23:05	BUY	1	GBP/USD	1.54848	12/20 7:14	1.56257	Low	$140
11/30/11 22:47	BUY	1	NZD/CHF	0.71161	12/8 8:47	0.72239	Low	$116
11/21/11 23:30	BUY	1	GBP/USD	1.56275	12/8 8:47	1.57585	Low	$130
10/31/11 22:58	BUY	2	AUD/USD	1.01956	12/2 7:56	1.02845	Low	$176
11/16/11 6:57	BUY	1	NZD/USD	0.76602	11/30 22:47	0.77802	Low	$119
11/16/11 6:58	BUY	1	AUD/JPY	77.968	11/30 22:47	79.352	Low	$177
9/21/11 23:00	BUY	2	NZD/CHF	0.70221	11/30 22:46	0.71094	Low	$189
11/24/11 9:33	BUY	1	NZD/CAD	0.77703	11/29 21:30	0.78889	Low	$114
11/24/11 9:32	BUY	1	AUD/CAD	1.01980	11/29 7:01	1.03109	Low	$109
11/24/11 9:32	BUY	1	AUD/CHF	0.89550	11/25 10:56	0.90957	Low	$150

Disclaimer: The content on this page is for educational purposes only and should not be construed in any way as trading advice. The risk of loss in online trading of stocks, Forex, options, and foreign equities is substantial.

| 10/27/11 23:07 | SELL | 1 | EUR/GBP | 0.88108 | 10/31 7:48 | 0.87475 | Low | $100 |

Have you noticed from the list of trades on the following pages that almost all of my trades (except four) are Long or Buy trades? When you buy a currency pair you control the downside risk as the value of a pair cannot fall below Zero, on the other hand the limit to the upside is infinite as the currency pair can keep on appreciating in your favor. When you sell a currency pair you are limiting your profits to a certain level as the currency pair cannot fall below Zero, and in addition you take on an infinite risk as the pair can keep on appreciating against your short trade.

Steps to Magical Trading:

1. As mentioned above we are only going to "Buy" a currency pair

2. We will limit ourselves to the "First World" currencies for our trades. The currencies we will use in our trading will be: AUD, CAD, CHF, EUR, GBP, JPY, NZD and USD. Any combinations of these currencies with one another only will be acceptable for our method.

3. Two more pairs which I will be trading in addition to the above mentioned combinations are ZAR/JPY, and NOK/JPY.

4. For every trade we open, our goal is to close it in a positive. Loss should not be part of our dictionary as we will like to keep our success rate as close to 100% as possible. Patience will be one of our virtues; there will be times when it might take a year or two for one of our open trades to become positive and reach a level where we are comfortable closing the trade.

5. Here I am going to demonstrate the steps for a $ 1000 account. You can apply the same principles to a $ 100, $ 10,000 or $ 100,000 accounts. As per our rules (page 11, Lots) we will trade only 100 units of a currency pair, no more no less, on an account with a deposit of $ 1000. Keep in mind it is your account and you are in-charge of your investing and armed with adequate knowledge I am confident that you will be able to control the risk. In-addition I expect that you will follow the rules, be disciplined and will not indulge in irrational high risk trades.

6. We control risk by proper position sizing. Always determine the proper units for your trade prior to entering the trade. Absolutely no short cuts here. If you have a trading account of $ 100 then any trade you open will have to be of 10 units only, where each pip move will equal 1/10th of a cent. For a $ 1000 account you enter a trade with 100 units where each pip move equals 1 cent. For a $ 2000 account you can open a trade with 200 units where each pip move equals 2 cents.

Disclaimer: The content on this page is for educational purposes only and should not be construed in any way as trading advice. The risk of loss in online trading of stocks, Forex, options, and foreign equities is substantial.

For a $ 10,000 account our entry will be of 1000 units with each pip move equaling 10 cents, so on and so forth. Position sizing is so vital to our trading that we cannot deviate from these principles.

7. Next review the 20 years monthly chart of the pair you plan to trade and review its price action to determine its current price level in relation to the highs and lows of the last 20 years. After reviewing the chart we should have answers to the following questions:

   a. Highest level reached within the last 20 years:
   b. Lowest level reached within the last 20 years:
   c. Price range of a pair in Pips over the last 20 years:
   d. Current price of the pair:
   e. Midpoint of range:
   f. Is the current price in the lower or upper half of the range:
   g Number of Pips from the current range to zero:

I am going to review five charts with you and determine the answers to the above questions. Our five charts will be USD/JPY, AUD/USD, EUR/USD, NZD/USD and USD/CHF

Chart # 1: USD/JPY

Monthly Chart: 1990 to 2013.

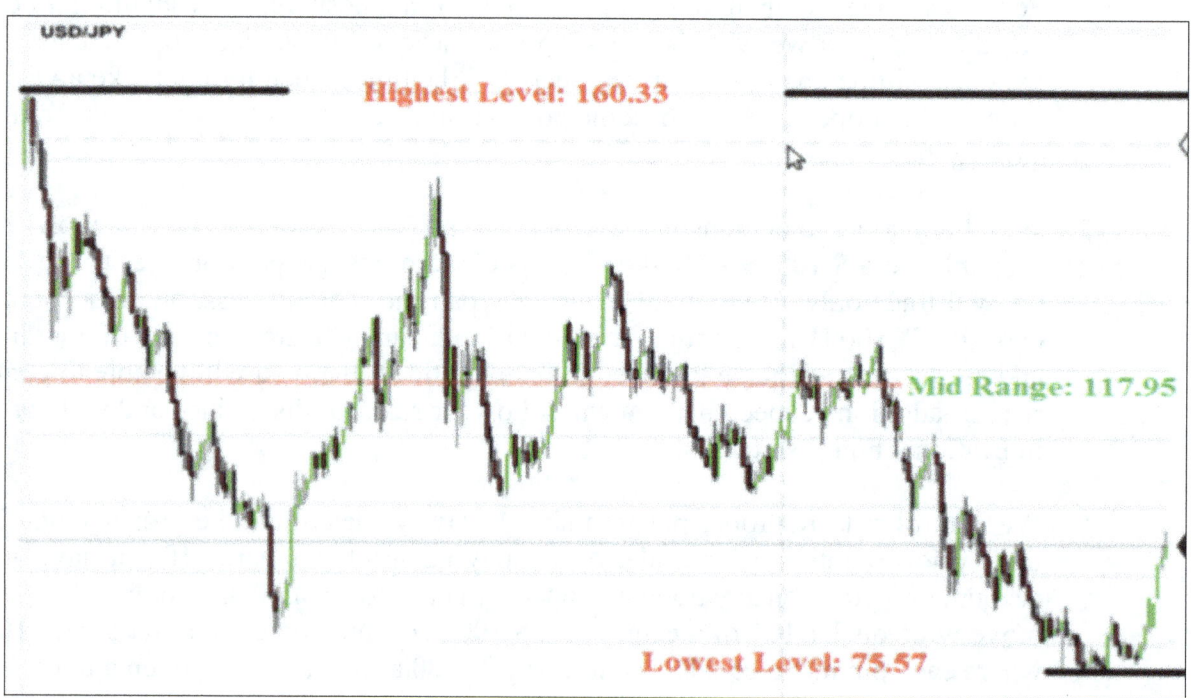

After reviewing this chart let us answer our questions listed above:

Disclaimer: The content on this page is for educational purposes only and should not be construed in any way as trading advice. The risk of loss in online trading of stocks, Forex, options, and foreign equities is substantial.

a. Highest level reached within the last 20 years: **160.33**
b. Lowest level reached within the last 20 years: **75.57**
c. Price range of a pair in Pips over the last 20 years: 16033-7557 = **8476**
d. Current price of the pair: **94.48**
e. Midpoint of the range: **117.95**
f. Is the current price in the lower or upper half of the range: **Lower Half**
g. Number of Pips from the current range to zero: **9448**

Here we have a good opportunity to go long the USD/JPY pair as the current price is well within the lower half of the last 20+ year price range and the number of pips from current price to zero are below 10,000.

Chart # 2: AUD/USD

Monthly Chart: 1990 to 2013.

After reviewing this chart let us answer our questions once again:

a. Highest level reached within the last 20 years: **1.1080**
b. Lowest level reached within the last 20 years: **0.4847**
c. Price range of a pair in Pips over the last 20 years: 11080 - 4847 = **6233**
d. Current price of the pair: **1.0447**
e. Midpoint of the range: **0.7963**
f. Is the current price in the lower or upper half of the range: **Upper Half**
g. Number of Pips from the current range to zero: **10447**

At these current levels the opportunity to go long the AUD/USD pair is not very enticing as the current price is well above the mid-range and is close to an all-time high for the last 20+ year price range and the numbers of pips from current price to zero are above 10,000. I will wait for the price to fall closer to the mid-range and also to fall below 10,000 pips to zero before considering a long trade on this pair. No long entry on AUD/USD for the moment.

Chart # 3: EUR/USD

Monthly Chart: 1990 to 2013.

After reviewing this chart let us answer our questions once again:

Disclaimer: The content on this page is for educational purposes only and should not be construed in any way as trading advice. The risk of loss in online trading of stocks, Forex, options, and foreign equities is substantial.

a. Highest level reached within the last 20 years: **1.6038**
b. Lowest level reached within the last 20 years: **0.8225**
c. Price range of a pair in Pips over the last 20 years: 16038 - 8225 = **7813**
d. Current price of the pair: **1.2970**
e. Midpoint of the range: **1.2131**
f. Is the current price in the lower or upper half of the range: **Upper Half**
g. Number of Pips from the current range to zero: **12970**

The current levels of the EUR/USD pair are in the upper half of the last 20+ year price range and the numbers of pips from current price to zero are above 10,000. Again the EUR/USD does not offer an exciting opportunity at the current levels. No long entry on EUR/USD for the moment.

Chart # 4: NZD/USD

Monthly Chart: 1990 to 2013.

After reviewing this chart let us answer our questions once again:

a. Highest level reached within the last 20 years: **0.8842**
   b. Lowest level reached within the last 20 years: **0.3900**
   c. Price range of a pair in Pips over the last 20 years: 8842 - 3900 = **4942**
   d. Current price of the pair: **0.8346**
   e. Midpoint of the range: **0.6371**
   f. Is the current price in the lower or upper half of the range: **Upper Half**
   g. Number of Pips from the current range to zero: **8346**

The current levels of the NZD/USD pair are in the upper half of the last 20+ year price range but the numbers of pips from current price to zero are below 10,000. I will consider a long NZD/USD if I don't get five low risk entries. Let us put NZD/USD entry on a hold for the moment.

Chart # 5: USD/CHF

Monthly Chart: 1990 to 2013.

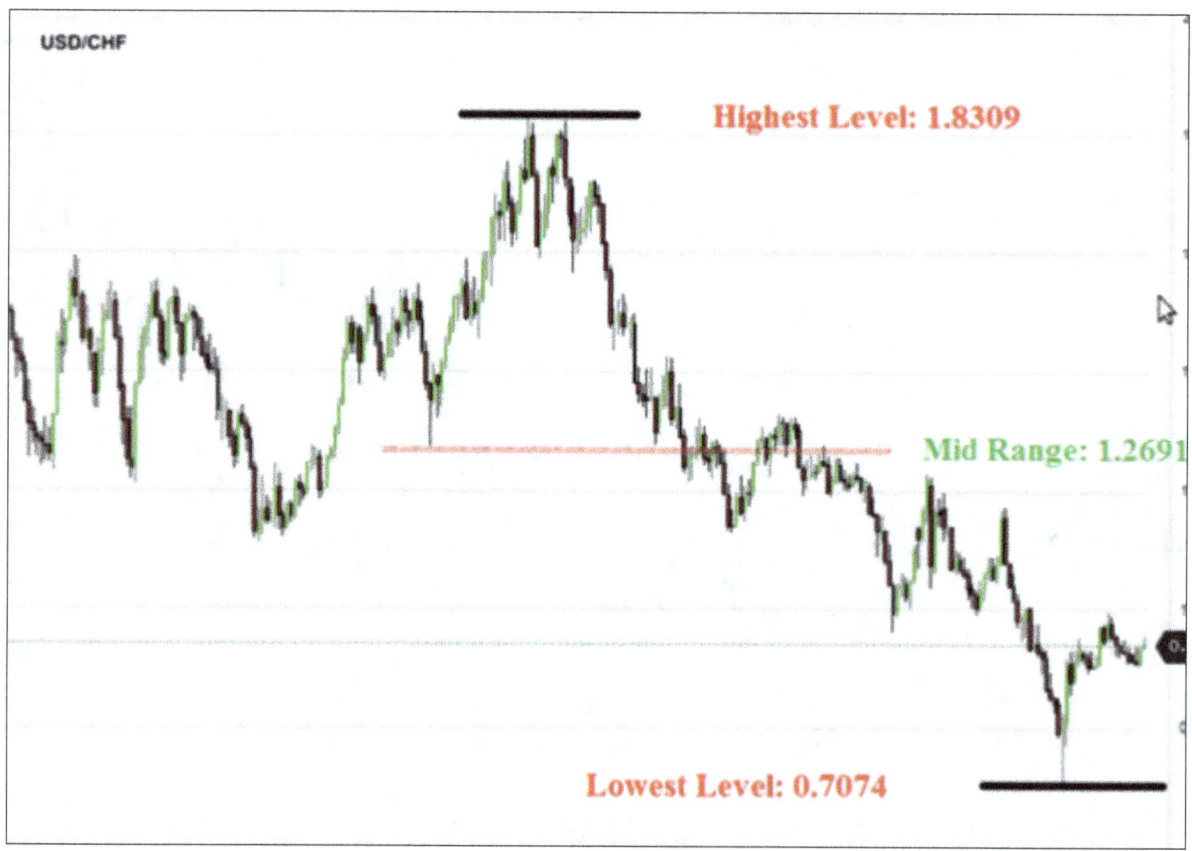

After reviewing this chart let us answer our questions listed above:

a. Highest level reached within the last 20 years: **1.8309**
b. Lowest level reached within the last 20 years: **0.7074**
c. Price range of a pair in Pips over the last 20 years: 18309-7074 = **11235**
d. Current price of the pair: **0.9410**
e. Midpoint of the range: **1.2691**
f. Is the current price in the lower or upper half of the range: **Lower Half**
g. Number of Pips from the current range to zero: **9410**

Here we have a good opportunity to go long the USD/CHF pair as the current price is well within the lower half of the last 20+ year price range and the number of pips from current price to zero are below 10,000.

8. After reviewing the combinations of all the currencies we selected, I am now ready to open 5 trades in the following order:

    a. First open a "Buy" trade on a <u>currency pair which is in the lower half of its last 20 year price range and the number of Pips from its current price to zero is below 10,000</u>. If you have five pairs in this category then open trades for those pairs. If you only find two pairs satisfying these criteria then open those two trades and move to the next option to get the other three pairs

    b. Our next choice is the <u>currency pair in the top half of its last 20 year price range and the number of Pips from its current price to zero is below 10,000</u>. If you are still short of five pairs after considering option a & b then move to option "c" for your remaining pairs

    c. The third choice is a <u>currency pair in the bottom half of its last 20 year price range and the number of Pips from its current price to zero is below 15,000</u>. After going through these three options you should be able to get your five pairs. If for some mysterious reason you are short one or two pairs then utilize ZAR/JPY and/ or NOK/JPY to complete the list

9. Now we have our five pairs and will open "Buy trades" on our live trading platform. Our golden rule is to stick to the position size discussed in step 6 and not to open more than 5 trades. You might have more than five pairs short listed based upon the options listed above but we will only select our top five pairs and keep the others as back up waiting to be executed once one of our five trades is closed out successfully.

10. Managing our open trades is a critical and intriguing part of Forex investing. I usually review my charts and trades for about 30-45 minutes in the morning at around 8:00 am (EST) and for another 30-45 minutes in the evening around 10:00 pm (EST). There is no specific reason for these times I just find these times convenient, you can select the time frame that suits you. My goal for these review sessions is to analyze the charts and have 2-3 back up trades ready by the end of each session and also to review my open trades and close any trade that meets my positive expectation. Forex market is open 24 hours a day for five day a week and the important sessions that follow each other on a daily basis are, "Asian Markets open from 2:00 pm EST to 1:00 am EST", "Tokyo session opens from 8:00 pm EST to 5:00 am EST", "London session opens from 3:00 am EST to 12:00 noon EST" and finally the "New York session opens at 8:00 am EST and closes at 5:00 pm EST". These sessions continue on a daily basis till 4:00 pm EST on Friday when the Forex market closes, the market opens back again at 5:00 pm EST on Sunday with the Asian session in progress.

I will review management of one open trade with you and we essentially use exactly the same steps for all our open trades. The steps are as follows:

> A. *If you find that, your trades are positive by over 100 Pips then close that trade.*
>
> - *Once a trade is closed then you can either open a new trade with a backup pair, in order to keep a total of 5 open trades at all times, or wait for the pair you just closed to retrace back within a day or two to the price you opened the initial trade at and then buy the same pair again.*
>
> - *If within a week the price does not retrace back then you can go ahead and open the backup trade, e.g. We bought USD/JPY at 0.9400 on 3/26/2013 evening, the pair is reviewed in the morning on 3/27/2013 and the price is now at 0.9480, the trade is up by 80 pips, the trade is kept open to be reviewed again in the evening on 3/27/2013.*
>
> - *Upon review we notice that the current price of USD/JPY is now 0.9580, our trade is positive with 180 pips therefore we immediately close the trade and book our profits.*
>
> - *Now we are left with 4 open trades we can take one of the following steps, either open a trade with a pair we have ready as a backup e.g. USD/CAD to again have 5 open trades or wait for USD/JPY to retrace back to 0.9400 in order to reopen the USD/JPY "Buy" trade.*
>
> - *If within a week the USD/JPY price does not retraces to 0.9400 then you can go ahead and open the backup trade.*

B. *If the trade is negative upon review, e.g. USD/CHF opened at 0.9000, then keep it open and wait for it to turn positive. This might take a few days or a few months; this is the time for our virtue of patience to be tested. Managing a negative trade is tedious and requires the following steps:*

- *Between -1 to -499 no action needed, requires review only*

- *Open another 100 units of USD/CHF if upon review this trade is over -500 pips negative(remember we are using a $ 1000 account)*

- *Now your trading platform will show six trades 2 for USD/CHF and 4 others*

- *These should still be considered as 5 open trades as 2 USD/CHF trades are counted as one trading complex*

- *Continue the review process, once the sum of these 2 USD/CHF trades is positive by over 100 pips then close the USD/CHF trading complex (2 trades) and immediately open one USD/CHF position e.g. first USD/CHF position opened at 0.9000, second USD/CHF position opened at 0.8500 the sum of these two positions will be 100 pips positive at 0.8800 therefore you close this complex and immediately open a new USD/CHF position as you are getting a better price for this pair at 0.8800 then your initial first trade at 0.9000. Manage this new trade if positive as listed in step "a" or as in step "b" if negative.*

- *If the price keeps on dropping after you have 2 open USD/CHF trades then open the third trade in that complex when the first USD/CHF trade is -1000 and the second USD/CHF trade is -500. Close when the sum of these three USD/CHF trading complex is +100 pips or more and immediately open a new USD/CHF position as you are getting a better price for this pair. Manage this new trade if positive as listed in step "a" or as in step "b" if negative.*

- *If the price still keeps on dropping after you have 3 open USD/CHF trades then open the fourth trade in that complex when the first USD/CHF trade is -2000 the second USD/CHF trade is -1500 and the third USD/CHF trade is -1000. Close when the sum of these four USD/CHF trading complex is +100 pips or more and immediately open a new USD/CHF position as you are getting a better price for this pair. Manage this new trade if positive as listed in step "a" or as in step "b" if negative.*

- *If the price still keeps on dropping after you have 4 open USD/CHF trades then open the fifth trade in that complex when the first USD/CHF trade is -4000 the second USD/CHF trade is -3500 the third USD/CHF trade is -3000 and the fourth USD/CHF trade is -2000. Close when the sum of these five USD/CHF trading complex is +100 pips or more and immediately open a new USD/CHF position as you are getting a better price for this pair. Manage this new trade if positive as listed in step "a" or as in step "b" if negative.*

- *Usually I will only have 5 positions open in a trading complex but if our other 4 pairs do not have more than two positions open in their complex then you can probably consider a sixth position in one of the trading complexes only if the first position of that complex is negative 6000 pips.*

C. *Follow step "a" if your trade is positive and follow steps in "b" if your trades are negative. Keep on repeating these steps, book your profits at above+ 100 pips and wait patiently for your negative complexes to turn positive.* **It is paramount that we do not have more than 13 positions (inclusive of positions within a trading complex)open at any given point.**

11. I have mentioned earlier that if we are unable to shortlist 5 pairs to trade then use ZAR/JPY and NOK/JPY. These two pairs are less volatile and the number of Pips from their current price to zero is well below 2000, therefore making these pairs low risk pairs to trade. If the trade turns negative and you have to add to these trading complexes then adjust the entries as follows:

✓ Add second position to the complex when the first position is at -100
✓ Add third position to the complex when the first position is at -200
✓ Add fourth position to the complex when the first position is at -400
✓ Add fifth position to the complex when the first position is at -600
✓ The rest of the trading strategy stays the same as listed under step 10

The Beginning:

I do not believe in conclusions, for me it is a new beginning after completion of a project. The purpose of this work is to create awareness, define concepts, describe strategies and lay down expectations about Forex Trading for the populous. This is a relatively new field which is still unknown to many individuals across the globe. I leave you with the principles and practical applications of Forex investing and hope that my trading strategies will arm you with the tools that will help carve a way towards successful Forex investing. This new journey will require Discipline, Patience and lots of Practice all the way through.

ANSWER TO QUIZZES

ANSWERS:

Chapter 1
Quiz A
1. 8333.33 Euros
2. 8333.33 Euros
3. 8333.33 Euros
4. $ 13,333.32
5. $ 13,333.32

Chapter 2
Quiz A
1. EUR/CHF
2. GBP/CHF
3. AUD/NZD
4. AUD/JPY
5. CHF/JPY

Quiz B
1. USD/HKD
2. TRY/JPY
3. NOK/JPY
4. EUR/GBP
5. EUR/AUD

Quiz C
1. Rand   ZAR
2. Euro   EUR
3. Krona   SEK
4. Forint   HUF
5. Lira   TRY

Quiz D
1. AUD   USD
2. USD   CAD
3. USD

4. GBP
5. Lost 20 pips

Quiz E
1. $ 1.60
2. 0.625 Pounds
3. 0.92 Swiss Francs
4. $ 1.08

Chapter 3
1. 2 pips
2. a. USD
   b. JPY
3. a. Profit
   b. 7 pips
4. a. micro
   b. 154 pips
   c. $15.40
   d. $0.10
5. a. 450 micro-lots
   b. $9360
   c. - 13 pips only
   d. $6750
6. a loss of 18 pips

Chapter 4
1. -18 pips

Chapter 5
Quiz 1
a. +292, +181, +282, +189, +353, +238, +82
b. 1617 pips
c. $16,170

Quiz 2
144 and 233

Quiz 3
Blue Candles

AU REVOIR

HAPPY TRADING TILL NEXT TIME

Disclaimer: The content on this page is for educational purposes only and should not be construed in any way as trading advice. The risk of loss in online trading of stocks, Forex, options, and foreign equities is substantial.

www.ingramcontent.com/pod-product-compliance
Lightning Source LLC
Chambersburg PA
CBHW051211290426
44109CB00021B/2417